# Quota

Sound And Vision

# Quotable Opera
## Aria ready for a laugh?

Compiled and Edited by
**Steve & Nancy Tanner**

ENRICO CARUSO - SIR PAOLO TOSTI - ANTONIO SCOTTI
**HELLO!**

Sound And Vision

# TABLE OF CONTENTS

# A
# PRELUDE
# WITH
# LEITMOTIFS

What are the three guys on our cover fussing
    about?
Caruso:     Maestro, the orchestra is too loud.
            My public won't hear me.
Toscanini: Caruso, I did you a favor.
Puccini:    Boys! Boys! Don't fight.

Welcome to the intimate world of things opera
people do, say, think and laugh about. We should be
grateful not only for the pleasures they give us
musically, but also for their colorful displays of human
cussedness. It would be hard to find any group more
temperamental than opera people, God bless them, or
more eager to poke fun at their profession and at each
other. Please note: in the competitive world of opera
quirky behavior, vainglorious grandstanding, slander,
imbroglios, deceit, jealousy and outright sabotage are
not abnormal.

Viennese General Manager and Conductor Franz
Schalk summed it all up:

"Every theater is a madhouse, but an opera theater is the ward for the incurables" to which American tenor Giuseppe Bentonelli (Joseph Horace Benton at birth) added,

"I have always found opera tinged with such a mild but persistent form of insanity that nothing surprises me any more."

To capture the essence of this glorious art, we have concentrated mainly on a few top-ranking composers, singers, critics and buffs, etc. A goodly number of the quotees have been close personal friends. Most of those quoted had very lively personalities and very lively opinions. We've included two quite controversial stars: Richard Wagner and Maria Callas. They reveled in controversy and in creating controversy.

We have many vivid memories, particularly of singers in their "anecdotage," in Munich, Milan and Florence in our homes or in theirs. If only we could relive some of those friendly, laughing visits to Titta Ruffo and the gatherings of old-time singers and musicians in the halls and bedrooms of the Casa Verdi. Many of our friends there had debuted before 1900. Several had sung with Caruso and other greats such as Toscanini, Puccini, Ruffo, Tamagno, et al.

ᘒᕼᕆᕦ

It's no secret that opera people are just like the rest of us, only more so.

Most are far bigger than we are, musically, emotionally, dramatically and often physically. Their home life is severely limited and their careers can force them into unconventional, self-centered, stressful and manic life styles. The euphoria of thunderous ovations and "Bravos," make up for many a personal sacrifice. They forget those hours and hours waiting in airports and gloomy railway stations. They forget those three-hour stints after tiring performances, signing autographs and then trying to appear happy, bouncy and buoyant at midnight parties where gushing socialites floor them with asinine comments, such as."Don't you just love operas? Well, I mean at least *some* of them?"

Some performers will do almost anything to get up onto the next rung on the professional ladder, A soprano from Dallas took off all her clothes. Her German voice guru claimed that was the only way he could tell if she was breathing properly. We know of a soprano who cut a quarter inch off her tongue after her coach said it was too long. Then, a famous fatty soprano allegedly ingested a live tapeworm so she could slim down fast.

Aside from first hand quotes which came from opera people we have known, most others came secondhand or, alternatively, from the writings of others. Also, to add spice, we quote from our own lectures and previous humor book, *Opera Antics & Anecdotes.* Composers shamelessly borrow from their own works. Why shouldn't we?

We dote on opera and opera people and pity those who do not share our enthusiasms

To end on a light note, we have reluctantly squelched pseudo-scholarly quotes on such dry topics as the influence of Igor Stravinsky, the Everly Brothers and Spike Jones on the following operas of Peter Schickele: *The Stoned Guest* (1967): *Hänsel and Gretel* and *Ted and Alice* (1972); *The Abduction of Figaro* (1984); *The Magic Bassoon* (1986).

Stephen and Nancy Tanner
July, 2003

# Let's Argue! What is Opera Anyhow?

An Opera is a Poetical Tale, or fiction, represented by Vocal and Instrumental Music adorn'd with Scenes, Machines and Dancing. The suppos'd Persons of the Musical Drama, are generally Supernatural, as Gods and Goddesses, and Heroes, which at least descended from them, and in due time are to be adopted into their number.

John Dryden

In this most dangerous of all art forms, so many elements are involved: acting, dancing, directing, designing, singing, and playing; so many things to go wrong. The miracle is that it succeeds as often as it does.

Raymond Leppard, conductor

Most operas are sexist, racist and politically very incorrect, what with plots glorifying male-dominated societies run by elitist gods, funky aristocrats and all manner of ego-maniacs bent on war, murder, rape, incest, kidnapping and every imaginable treachery and intrigue.

From *Opera Antics & Anecdotes*

Opera is the visible and audible projection of the power, wealth, and taste of the society which supports it.

DONALD JAY GROUT

[In America the money for producing opera has come from]... the wealthy, fashionable classes, who, even if not caring especially for, nor appreciating deeply the music, find it a peculiar and valuable social feature.

JOSIAH CLEVELAND CADY,
ARCHITECT OF THE OLD MET BUILDING

In Europe when a wealthy woman has an affair with a conductor, the result is sometimes a baby, but in America the result can be a whole symphony orchestra [or an opera production!]

EDGAR VARESE

Opera is strictly a matter of business. It's the selection of famous voices for fashionable ears. It has little bearing to art as art.

MAURICE GRAU, DIRECTOR AT THE MET

[Opera is] the most rococo and degraded of all art forms.

WILLIAM MORRIS, 19TH CENTURY ENGLISH POET

The opera... is to music what a bawdy house is to a cathedral.

H. L. MENCKEN, AMERICAN AUTHOR & CRITIC

... it is one of the most magnificent and expensive diversions the wit of man can invent.

JOHN EVELYN

Music hath charms to soothe the savage breast, to soften rocks, or bend a knotty oak.

WILLIAM CONGREVE

Music is the shorthand of emotion. Emotions which let themselves be described in words with such difficulty, are directly conveyed to man in music, and in that is power and significance.

LEO TOLSTOY

Music hath charms to soothe the savage beast, but I'd try a revolver first.

JOSH BILLINGS, AMERICAN 19TH CENTURY HUMORIST

Opera is the most wonderful convergence of all the arts… It's music, poetry, graphic arts, lights, and technology all creating an experience that may be thrilling, riveting, laughable, or silly, boring, awful… Opera is one-stop shopping where you partake in all the arts.

ROBERT BROCK

… try to concentrate on the music. The music is the truth of opera.

ANN PATCHETT

English poets could never accept the idea of a *normal* man expressing himself in song (for instance, in an aria).

EDWARD J. DENT

An exotick, irrational entertainment.

DR. SAMUEL JOHNSON

… what's rational about an art form in which some Mimi in a massive muumuu is supposed to be wasting away to nothing, an art form where tiny tenors romance strapping sopranos and all the singers convey their secret emotions and innermost thoughts at full blast to the seats in the very back of the hall?

DAVID W. BARBER, IN *OPERA ANTICS & ANECDOTES*

13

… to hear a parcel of Italian eunuchs, like so many cats, squall out somewhat you don't understand.

THOMAS BAKER IN *TUNBRIDGE WALKS* 1703

Going to the opera, like getting drunk, is a sin that carries its own punishment with it.

HANNAH MOORE

There were others… who would have said… opera was a collection of nonsensical cat screechings, that they would rather pass three hours in a dentist's chair. These were the ones who wept openly now, the ones who had been so mistaken.

ANN PATCHETT

For the magic of opera depends on more than the waving of a wand… on more than the skill of the stage director. It involves hundreds of people carrying on their tasks in four languages, driven to peak efficiency after sunset.

MARY ELLIS PELTZ

I think that's why people applaud for half an hour at opera, and almost never applaud for half an hour at plays. It's not that the experience of a play is any less exciting… It's just that their adrenaline and emotions are high at opera.

SIR PETER HALL, ENGLISH THEATRE DIRECTOR

A rare, perfect, blooperless performance astonishes the cast and orchestra even more than the public.

OVERHEARD BY THE EDITOR

… what we need is music of the earth, everyday music… music one can live in like a house.

JEAN COCTEAU, FRENCH WRITER & FILM DIRECTOR

The Golden Age of opera is always the era *before* that of the questioner.

HAROLD ROSENTHAL

Down the ages, parents have been claiming their children were born a bit too late to hear the last Golden Age of Opera. If their claim were correct, when opera was born centuries ago, like Venus from the wave, it must have been perfect and has been deteriorating ever since.

THE EDITOR *OPERA ANTICS & ANECDOTES*

We have these huge dinosaurs all over the planet, these opera houses with all this neat stuff in them.

PHILIP GLASS, AMERICAN COMPOSER

… as the popularity of most contemporary opera is scant, the problem of the supremacy of words has virtually become moot, and the librettist himself may be a dying breed.

WILLIAM WEAVER

Bed is the poor man's opera.

AN OLD ITALIAN SAYING

# THAT'S SUPPOSED TO BE ACTING?!!?

You have a beautiful voice, Merrill... You're a great baritone. But *don't* be a baritone, be a *father.*

ARTURO TOSCANINI TO ROBERT MERRILL REHEARSING
GIORGIO GERMONT IN *TRAVIATA*

Observing your grave, deliberate motion, I was reminded, Mr. X, of that estimable quadruped, the hedgehog.

SIR THOMAS BEECHAM TO THE TENOR IN *DIE MEISTERSINGER*

The chorus violated all traditions of the Italian stage by taking an intelligent part in what was going on.

MAX MARETZEK

One... critic once characterized his [Sherrill Milnes'] Don Giovanni as having all the aristocratic bearing and dangerous erotic appeal of an Iowa college frat-house stud... his generalized performances seldom amounted to more than one-dimensional vocalized portraits.

PETER G. DAVIS IN *THE AMERICAN SINGER*

Butterfly is fifteen, Manon is sixteen, and Salome is hardly older than Lolita; I haven't seen any prima donnas who qualify. Luckily, opera rises above such matters. *Everything* in opera is larger than life.

BEVERLY SILLS

When I have a fat tenor.., I cannot get inspired. In *Trovatore* when I sing *Sei tu dal ciel disceso* with Franco [Corelli] one really feels he has descended from heaven. Most other tenors could have dropped down from anywhere.

ANTONIETTA STELLA

16

... I feel a bit silly playing an eighteen-year-old girl. After all, I *am* a grandmother now, and I don't think a granny is supposed to make a living by getting up in front of thousands of people, pretending to be a teen-ager!

JOAN SUTHERLAND, ON SINGING *LUCIA DI LAMERMOOR*

It once took two and a half hours to make me up as Elizabeth I in her sixties and only a half-hour to turn me into a seventeen-year-old Manon. Now it's the other way round... That's the way the cookie crumbles.

BEVERLY SILLS

An opera singer's only idea of acting is to stand at the footlights in the middle of the stage and wave his arms alternately.

RICHARD WAGNER

... opera, ... it's a supertheater, theater raised that much higher. And when the acting is good, as it sometimes is, then it's better than good — it's great. We have no acting to compare with operatic acting when it's great.

TONY RANDALL

Florentine tenor Giuseppe Fancelli's acting consisted of stretching his hands toward the audience with his five fingers spread, which earned him the nickname "Signor Five-and-five-makes-ten."

JOHN GUALIANI

... it's either something you're born with or you're not. You can teach somebody how to kick off with the upstage leg rather than the downstage one, and not to cross over badly, and how to hold a fan... but if you haven't got that in-built desire to get up there and show off...

ISOBEL BUCHANAN

17

As a rule, all you could see would be a couple of people, one of them standing still, and the other catching flies.

MARK TWAIN ON ACTING IN WAGNERIAN OPERAS

I wanted to show that there is an alternative way of portraying Tosca to Callas's. Callas, who began the operatic revolution that has turned opera into believable theatre, was unique and inimitable. What is the point of trying to ape her?

EVA MARTON

[Like Callas] I, too, have tried to do my bit to promote the idea of opera as believable theatre, the way the composers visualized it.

RENATA SCOTTO

You've got to have a certain type of personality to stand up there and vocalise from your deepest feelings... It's a disadvantage to be too intellectual about it.

PETER KNAPP, BARITONE & PRODUCER

I think it is the sound of singing that people want when they come to the opera. If they want a good dramatic performance, they should go to a straight play.

DAME JOAN SUTHERLAND

[In *Otello*] Mario del Monaco, who had a magnificent physique, entered stripped to the waist. But his Negro makeup ended at his neck. That was, without doubt, the single biggest laugh I have ever heard in a theater.

TONY RANDALL IN *WHICH REMINDS ME*

The typical Wagnerian soprano looks like an ox, she moves like a cart horse, she stands like a haystack.

ERNEST NEWMAN

## COMPOSERS PONDERING THEIR ART
### AND EACH OTHER

An orchestra in the hands of an Italian composer is nothing other than a monstrous guitar which he uses to accompany arias.

RICHARD WAGNER

When Rossini went to Paris for the first time, his rivals nicknamed him Signor Baccano (Mr. Uproar), Signor Crescendo, or Signor Chiassoni (Mr. Big Noises). Rossini laughed at the names they coined for him and observed contentedly, "My rivals would be very happy indeed if they could make as much noise around town as I have."

ADOLFO LAPPINI IN *CINQUECENTO E UNA CURIOSITÀ MUSICALI*

If it had been in my power to place a barrel of powder under the Louvois Theater, and explode it into the air, with all that it contained, during a performance of *The Thieving Magpie* or *The Barber of Seville*, I swear I would not have shrunk from the task.

HECTOR BERLIOZ

I heard *Rosenkavalier* for the first time after the war and I confess I prefer Gilbert and Sullivan. Sullivan has a sense of timing and punctuation which I have never been able to find in Strauss.

IGOR STRAVINSKY

It is better to make a piece of music than to perform one, better to perform one than to listen to one, better to listen to one than to misuse it as a means of distraction, entertainment, or acquisition of culture.

JOHN CAGE

19

He [Wagner] didn't only compose, he built an opera house and created the conditions in which his own music could be performed.

PIERRE BOULEZ, CONDUCTOR & COMPOSER

A composer should never write unless he is acquainted with the demands for his work. The times for constant composing for one's own satisfaction are probably gone forever.

PAUL HINDEMITH [OH YEAH, PAUL? GUESS AGAIN]

For opera buffa, on the other hand, he [Johann Simon Mayer] shows all the elephantine gaiety of a good, dull-witted burgher.

M. H. B. STENDHAL, AUTHOR

*Boris Godunov* is Mussorgsky's only completed opera in about ten attempts.

THE OXFORD DICTIONARY OF THE OPERA

What is there for me in Mussorgsky? I didn't hear…a single idea or a single word expressed with real profundity of understanding. Everything about him is flabby and colorless. To me he seems a perfect idiot.

VLADIMIR STASSOV, IN HISTORY OF RUSSIAN MUSIC, COMPOSER

Mussorgsky is practically an idiot.

MILI BALAKIREV, COMPOSER [IBID]

As a boy, Mendelssohn wrote a number of operas ... these early works include some delightful and effective numbers, that do not, however, suggest a larger dramatic gift.

THE OXFORD DICTIONARY OF THE OPERA

[Liszt's] sole completed opera was *Don Sanche*... the work shows, unsurprisingly, little sign of individuality but includes some effective music (including for a storm).

IBID

I have been listening to you for two hours and YOU have said nothing to ME!

LUIGI CHERUBINI, AFTER LISTENING TO AN OPERA BY
HIS PUPIL FROMENTAL HALEVY, WHO ASKED,
"MAESTRO, HAVE YOU NOTHING TO SAY TO ME?"

Appetite is for the stomach what love is for the heart... Eating, loving, singing, and digesting are the four acts of the comic opera known as life.

GIOACCHINO ROSSINI IN *501 CURIOSITÀ MUSICALI*

Many times I thought of getting down to work again, a good libretto would perhaps have persuaded me, but I never found one. I was offered two or three versions of *Joan of Arc*. In one she was loved and in the other she was IN love. What does love have to do with the legend of *Joan of Arc*?

...When a plot does not offer the fascination of love you should put it aside and don't think about it any more. And that's what I did.

ROSSINI, WHEN ASKED WHY HE STOPPED WRITING OPERAS
IN 1829 AFTER *GUILLAUME TELL* [IBID]

21

Whoever has heard one of my operas knows them all.

IBID

Rossini: How's it going, dear colleague, with your *L'Africaine*?
Meyerbeer: I'm making some corrections.
Rossini: How lucky you are that you still have time to make corrections! I, instead, am erasing and making cuts.

*CINQUECENTO E UNA CURIOSITÀ MUSICALI*
EDITED BY ADOLFO LAPPINI

Operas by women are like their children: you're never sure who the father was.

GIOACCHINO ROSSINI

[Schubert was] another composer whose theatrical sense was insufficient to write beyond the pretty.

WILLIAM FREGOSI, TECHNICAL COORDINATOR
FOR THEATER ARTS AT M.I.T

First operas, like first puppies, should all be drowned!

CARL MARIA VON WEBER TO SCHUBERT AFTER
PERUSING SCHUBERT'S FIRST OPERAS

Beethoven's theater music is not one-quarter as vital and telling as that of Mozart.

SIR THOMAS BEECHAM, CONDUCTOR

Take this imbecile off my hands!

JACQUES MEYERBEER, RECOMMENDING RICHARD WAGNER
TO THE HEAD OF THE PARIS OPERA

I have wept only twice in my life, once when I dropped a truffled turkey into Lake Como, and when I heard Mozart for the first time.

Gioacchino Rossini
[many versions of this quote exist]

Herr Hindemith, where are the toilets in this place?

Conductor Otto Klemperer, during the question
period at the end of a long, dull, pedantic
lecture on esthetics by Hindemith

As to what happens when I compose, I really haven't the faintest idea.

Samuel Barber

You ask how I compose. I compose sitting down.

Pyotr Tchaikovsky, answering a woman's query

Music must become so complex and intricate as to eliminate automatically all dilettantism.

Ferruccio Busoni [Some music has done just that, Ferruccio,
and has not only eliminated dilettantism,
but also many listeners]

I defy any one to record that Mr. Berlioz has respected any glorious tradition, whether of melody, rhythm or human voice. Melody usually escapes from him, and if, perchance, he catches one, he would torture it with a barbarous glee, just as a bad boy would pluck the feathers of a live bird.

Blaze de Bury, French critic (1838) quoted in
*Sharps and Flats* by Max Maretzek

And Berlioz! Did he not in his letters call the composer of *Norma* and *Puritani* a "petit polisson" (a little blackguard) "by the name of Bellini?" and the composer of *Saffo* (Paccini) "miserable eunuch?" and did he not say that the music of Donizetti's opera *The Elixir of Love* made him "shiver as if insects were crawling over his body?" Even Haydn said of Beethoven, that "he is a great pianist and nothing more." Handel said that "his cook was just a good a musician as Gluck."

MAX MARETZEK IN *SHARPS AND FLATS* (1890)

The music of Wagner imposes mental tortures that only algebra has the right to inflict.

PAUL DE SAINT-VICTOR

Wagner's music is better than it sounds.

MARK TWAIN
[NO QUOTE BOOK IS COMPLETE WITHOUT THIS ANCIENT CHESTNUT]

Wagner is Berlioz without the melody.

DANIEL AUBER

Is Wagner a human being at all? Is he not rather a disease?

FRIEDRICH NIETZSCHE

Parsifal is Christianity arranged for Wagnerians.

FRIEDRICH NIETZCHE

A sort of chromatic moan.

HECTOR BERLIOZ ON *TRISTAN UND ISOLDE*

So much C major!

ARTURO TOSCANINI ON *DIE MEISTERSINGER*

There are still so many beautiful things to be said in C major.

SERGEI PROKOFIEV

Verdi needs beautiful singing or the audience is bored to death — but Wagner has the orchestra, and the conductor can play it like a symphony, without the voice.

THOMAS STEWART

Who but Wagner could make a shoemaker the hero of an opera!

DR. RUDOLF SCHNEIDER, ON *Die Meistersinger*

[Wagner] could write of "deeds of music made visible" – but he could also laugh at how this could dwindle down to "ladies being hoisted to the roof by strings attached to their bottoms."

RICHARD DYER, MUSIC CRITIC

As the comedian Anna Russell liked to remind us, the woman Siegfried wakes up to is his aunt.

BIRGIT NILSSON

Create for me something that will make the world weep.

GIACOMO PUCCINI, TO HIS LIBRETTIST FOR *Turandot*

What a pity that Wagner means to set it (*Lohengrin*) to music himself. His musical gifts are not equal to that.

FERDINAND HILLER

25

*Lohengrin* makes perfect sense once you understand that the title character was gay. After all, here's a guy on his wedding night and all he wants to do is talk. Looks to me like he is VERY nervous about having sex with his wife – he just keeps putting things off, and then he seizes on a flimsy pretext to leave her so he doesn't have to go through with it. A straight guy would have just thrown Elsa in the sack and made her squeal to the point that she wouldn't care WHAT his name was. No doubt his father, Parsifal, was concerned about Lohengrin turning into a nancy-boy so he sent him off to do some fighting and get married. I think Lohengrin was tickled pink to get out of his marital duties and go hang out with the guys at Montsalvat, singing show-tunes and designing art deco grail containers.

MY COLLEAGUE, THE AUTHOR, REQUESTED ANONYMITY

Asked why he did not leave Germany during the Nazi era, Strauss said Germany had fifty-six opera houses, the United States had two. 'It would have reduced my income.' [Richard couldn't count]

VIA MRS. MICKEY DOVE

Through singing, (opera) must make you weep, shudder, die.

VINCENZO BELLINI

[Puccini was] more like the heir to Verdi than any of his rivals.

GEORGE BERNARD SHAW

… the composer is still my most important teacher. Search Puccini's score, and you find the meaning behind the melodies.

RENATA SCOTTO, SOPRANO

26

If only I could be a purely symphonic writer!... But that was not for me... Almighty God touched me with His little finger and said: 'Write for the theatre — mind, only for the theatre.'

GIACOMO PUCCINI
[FROM A LETTER TO LIBRETTIST GIUSEPPE ADAMI]

... into the midst of so much Chinese mannerism... do a little of what Shakespeare often does, when he brings in three or four extraneous types who drink, use bad language, and speak ill of the King.

GIACOMO PUCCINI
TO GIUSEPPE ADAMI, HIS LBRETTIST FOR *TURANDOT*

... [at] a rehearsal of *Amahl and the Night Visitors*... the only spectators... were Arturo Toscanini and Olin Downes ... when the crippled Amahl offers his crutch to the Christ Child and is suddenly able to walk, Toscanini and Downes broke down and wept..

GIAN CARLO MENOTTI QUOTED IN *A LITTLE NIGHT MUSIC*

You write music from the heart, not from the head, as all other composers unfortunately do these days.

ARTURO TOSCANINI TO GIAN CARLO MENOTTI [ IBID]

Repetitous, rhetorical and da-di-dum.

PIERRE BOULEZ ON VERDI

Passion, passion, passion, passion, unimportant which, but passion!

GIUSEPPE VERDI, TO HIS LIBRETTIST

Music begins where the words end.

JOHANN WOLFGANG VON GOETHE, AUTHOR AND ESTHETE

... I cut scenes, often with a bleeding heart, out of my operas. That was Wagner's tragedy. He wouldn't cut his words. A composer must not hesitate to be a surgeon and operate on himself.

GIAN CARLO MENOTTI

To write good opera you must have the courage not to write.

GIUSEPPE VERDI

*Le Roi S'amuse* is the greatest subject and perhaps the greatest drama of modern times. Triboulet [*Rigoletto*] is a character worthy of Shakespeare! This is a subject that cannot fail.

VERDI TO LIBRETTIST F. M. PIAVE

The subject is great, immense, and there is a character who is one of the greatest creations of which the theater of all countries and all times can boast. The subject is *Le Roi S'amuse* and the character I speak of is Triboulet. Run throughout the city, and find a person of influence who can get permission to do *Le Roi S'amuse*. Don't sleep. Get moving. Hurry.

GIUSEPPE VERDI TO LIBRETTIST PIAVE REGARDING *RIGOLETTO*

I wonder if you realize how much work you've thrown my way?

SOPRANO CLAUDIA MUZIO ADDRESSING A PORTRAIT OF VERDI

For some operas you can accept a voice of not absolute beauty — if it is well used and he is an artist and interpreter, it will work. But for Verdi you need all this plus the essential sound.

CARLO MARIA GIULINI, CONDUCTOR

[*Aida* is] no longer art...(but) a pleasure party, a hunt.

GIUSEPPE VERDI, ON THE LAVISH FIRST PRODUCTION IN EGYPT

Meantime Mozart's opera *The Marriage of Figaro* was shown on the stage: and in spite of the doubts, reserves, and head shakings of the other maestros and of their partisans ... it was a success with the public, while the Sovereign and other real connoisseurs judged it a thing sublime not to say divine.

LORENZO DA PONTE

Though gifted with talents superior perhaps to those of any other composer in the world, past, present or future, Mozart had, thanks to the intrigues of his rivals, never been able to exercise his divine genius in Vienna, and was living there unknown and obscure, like a priceless jewel buried in the bowels of the earth and hiding the refulgent excellence of its splendors.

LORENZO DA PONTE

Had this man [Mozart] lived, none of the rest of us would earn a crust of bread for our operas.

ANTONIO SALIERI, MOZART'S RIVAL COMPOSER IN VIENNA

Salieri, who was, to tell the bare truth, a most cultivated and intelligent man.

LORENZO DA PONTE

I love the other Mozart operas, but I don't think it's always easy to identify with all the characters.

FEDERICA VON STADE, MEZZO SOPRANO
COMMENTING ON *THE MARRIAGE OF FIGARO*

*Figaro* seems to me very modern, both in subject and style. The one and only Wolfgang Amadeus Mozart succeeded in creating a universe that will seem real forever.

IBID

To imitate reality may be a good thing, but to invent reality is better — much better.

GIUSEPPE VERDI

Composers shouldn't think too much — it interferes with their plagiarism.

HOWARD DIETZ

A good composer does not imitate, he steals.

IGOR STRAVINSKY, AN ADMITTED OPERA-TUNIST

A friend:  Is that one of your tunes?
Rossini:  Not yet!

APOCRYPHAL, WHILE STROLLING, ROSSINI AND A FRIEND
HEARING MUSIC COMING FROM A WINDOW IN PARIS

# Toscanini, Beecham, Other Conductors and Semi-conductors

Conductors, the glamour boys of music.
OSCAR LEVANT, PIANIST & CRITIC, IN *A SMATTERING OF IGNORANCE*

The conductor is the most to be feared of all performers. A singer can ruin only his own part, but the conductor of the orchestra can ruin everything.
HECTOR BERLIOZ, COMPOSER

Why do we have to have all these third-rate foreign conductors around — when we have so many second-rate ones of our own?
SIR THOMAS BEECHAM

I think you have to be born a conductor… the *feeling* of conducting has to be inside you, it's something no one can teach you. I wasn't born a tenor… But conducting… that's a skill you either have or you don't.
PLACIDO DOMINGO WHO STUDIED CONDUCTING AT JUILLIARD

... when you conduct opera, you've got two sets of forces to control at once, the singers 'upstairs' and the players 'downstairs'.

PLACIDO DOMINGO

The question is one of domination — whether the conductor dominates the orchestra, or the orchestra dominates the conductor.

OSCAR LEVANT

... at the Paris Opera in Lully's time, the composer set the tempo by pounding a stick on the floor — an aural distraction it's hard for us to imagine an audience tolerating.

JAMES LEVINE

I managed to make myself understood (Italians usually do) by means of vivid gesticulation and a fluent conglomeration of several languages.

LUIGI ARDITI, CONDUCTOR & COMPOSER

When I am standing in front of a grand orchestra and have drunk half a bottle of champagne, then I conduct like a young god. Otherwise, I am nervous and tremble and feel insecure.

JEAN SIBELIUS, A PROBLEM DRINKER
IN *MORE LOVE LIVES OF THE GREAT COMPOSERS*

He [the conductor] should understand and respect other musicians and singers who may have personalities different from his own, This is especially true when working with an opera where so many other people are involved.

CLAUDIO ABBADO, QUOTED IN *MAESTRO*

New York Philharmonic Concert Master: You've had us rehearse this overture four times. What are we doing wrong, Maestro,
Conductor Andre Kostelanetz: If I only knew, I'd tell you.

VIA BRUCE SURTEES

Running a symphony orchestra is a quarter the amount of trouble of running an opera house.

GEORG SOLTI, IN MAESTRO BY HELENA MATHEOPOULOS

In the beginning, there was rhythm.

HANS VON BÜLOW, CONDUCTOR

The conductor must be entirely independent of the management and must be given complete musical responsibility, regardless of the committee, the management and the public. He should choose the chorus master, to whom not only the music instruction should be entrusted, but also the stage instruction. The chorus master, or his assistant, should further be obliged to dress in costume during performances and sing with the choruses.

GIUSEPPE VERDI

A good conductor must have two requirements: to be able to give the right time clearly and unmistakably and to possess personality.

RICHARD WAGNER

Two essentials for a conductor's success are a fine set of tails and a rich wife.

POPULAR ADAGE BACKSTAGE

33

Rhythmic wriggles of Leonard Bernstein's rear end showed the tempo he wanted.

AN ORCHESTRA MEMBER

We saw Joan Sutherland lead the orchestra with little movements of her jutting chin to show her conductor husband the tempo she wanted.

AN AUDIENCE MEMBER

When I conduct, I conduct, and when I sing, I sing... perhaps I have more sympathy for what a conductor has to do than some singers.

PLACIDO DOMINGO

Modern music is three farts and a raspberry orchestrated.

SIR JOHN BARBIROLLI, CONDUCTOR

Soprano:  Oh Maestro, I've taken that score to bed with me every night.
Thomas Beecham:  Well, soon we shall have the immaculate conception.

JEF OLSON, OPERA DIECTOR

... we are confronted with the paradoxical situation that, while never before have there been so many musicians who are credited with impeccable mechanical excellence, there have also never been so many dull and uninspiring interpreters.

SIR THOMAS BEECHAM

You learn according to the rules and then you forget them.

TULLIO SERAFIN, CONDUCTOR

I should always prefer not to see the orchestra at all, and certainly not the conductor whose distracting and self-exhibiting gestures are the public nuisance of almost all opera houses.

EDWARD J. DENT, MUSICOLOGIST

Listen to your singer, the tempo is the one which is right for her.

TULLIO SERAFIN, GIVING ADVICE TO RICHARD BOYNINGE

… you can occasionally have a child prodigy pianist or violinist, but never a real child prodigy conductor.

PLACIDO DOMINGO

I started my career as a violinist. When that became too difficult, I became a viola player. When that became to difficult, I became a conductor. And when I can no longer do anything, I will become a critic.

PIERRE MONTEUX

There are no boring roles. There are only boring singers.

SARAH CALDWELL, CONDUCTOR & PRODUCER

The singers think they are going to be heard, and I'm going to make jolly well certain that they aren't.

SIR THOMAS BEECHAM PREPARING *ELEKTRA* FOR COVENT GARDEN

There are many cardinals, but Toscanini is pope.

RICHARD STRAUSS

They said Toscanini had no repertoire. No repertoire?
He knew every opera. Every one. Every note of every
one. Mon Dieu, what that man had in his head!

PIERRE MONTEUX, CONDUCTOR

The Slave Driver — Napoleon — Maestro Tosca-no-no
— the Sorcerer

A FEW ORCHESTRA-INVENTED NICKNAMES FOR ARTURO TOSCANINI

Many orchestra players considered Toscanini cruel, in-
flexible, and even petty... I know of no man, however,
who does not consider him the greatest conductor, *qua
conductor*, with whom he has ever played.

OSCAR LEVANT

Toscanini conducted 53 operas from memory. He led
almost 500 non-operatic works by 175 composers, also
without a score

THE EDITOR IN *OPERA ANTICS & ANECDOTES*

God tells me how the music should sound, but you
stand in the way.

ARTURO TOSCANINI TO AN ERRANT TRUMPET PLAYER

The score requests *con amore,* and what are you doing?
You are playing it like a married man.

ARTURO TOSCANINI IN REHEARSAL

I hate you all because you destroy my dreams!

ARTURO TOSCANINI TO THE ORCHESTRA IN REHEARSAL

My orchestra are simply assassins.

ARTURO TOSCANINI

By their basses ye shall know them.

HANS VON BÜLOW

You sing. I will follow you.

ARTURO TOSCANINI TO TENOR JAN PEERCE

Look to the words and the voice will carry itself.

ARTURO TOSCANINI

That S cut in your violin case stands for STUDY!!!

ARTURO TOSCANINI TO AN ERRING VIOLINIST

One unfortunate, a violinist, was invariably target of his criticism... During a visit... to another city Toscanini, in a rage, placed the blame squarely on his *bête noire* in the orchestra even though the musician had remained in New York, ill.

OSCAR LEVANT

I also listened to that tenor Peirani, whose grandiose bestial ignorance frightened me. He is ... a cretin of the highest order.

ARTURO TOSCANINI IN A LETTER TO HIS FUTURE WIFE,
CARLA DE MARTINI

Too bad he never learned to read a full orchestra score, and conducted using only a piano voice score.

ARTURO TOSCANINI ON HIS MANHATTAN
OPERA RIVAL, CLEOFONTE CAMPANINI

That Russian boor... Such a bad conductor, and the orchestra plays so well.

ARTURO TOSCANINI ON SERGE KOUSSEVITSKY

An Italian peasant... Very good for Italian opera.

SERGE KOUSSEVITSKY ON ARTURO TOSCANINI

A gifted amateur.

ARTURO TOSCANINI ON WILHELM FURTWÄNGLER

I begin where Toscanini leaves off.

WILHELM FURTWÄNGLER ON ARTURO TOSCANINI

A crazy nut!

ARTURO TOSCANINI ON GUSTAV MAHLER

That clown!

ARTURO TOSCANINI ON LEOPOLD STOKOWSKI

The Beckmesser of conductors.

ARTURO TOSCANINI ON KARL MUCK

Schonberg is out of tune with my ears.

ARTURO TOSCANINI

[Toscanini] never conceded that there even *was* a La
Scala when he wasn't there.

JEROME TOOBIN

You know, Jerry, Maestro [Toscanini] has never invited
me to Riverdale any more since my divorce. He absolutely refuses to have divorced people as social guests.
He is a great believer in the family. So I am out.

EUGENE ORMANDY CONDUCTOR, TO JEROME TOOBIN

I slept with that woman for seven years. Wouldn't you
think she'd remember that I hate fish?

ARTURO TOSCANINI ON BEING SERVED CAVIAR AT
DINNER IN THE HOME OF ELDERLY SOPRANO GERALDINE FARRAR

*Wozzeck* was written by a Chinaman from Vienna.

GIGLIOLA GALLI

... Ramses II, whom they call The Great... He lived to be 85, reigned for 67 years, and as a pastime fathered 162 children — 111 males and 51 females. Among his many wives were three of his sisters and two of his daughters. Not bad! Were morals back then better or worse than today? Who knows!!!

Arturo Toscanini in a letter from Egypt

You know, there's a fine line between artistry and shit. Not that what you're doing is shit, but it's close to it.

Conductor to the orchestra from
*FW Conductor Funnies*

Now forget all the nasty things I said and play naturally.

*FW Conductor Funnies*

Play as if you were musicians.

*FW Conductor Funnies*

Music should be beautiful from the aesthetic point of view, and should have a profound meaning. Superficial music, and music which is not beautiful, doesn't interest me.

Claudio Abbado

[A young conductor told a soprano who had asked for more time in a certain passage that it was *he* who decided where and for how long she could breathe], which, needless to say, is absolute rubbish!

KARL BÖHM

If the tenor (in *Otello*) rants at every climax, the audience will start to yawn!

JAMES LEVINE

Wagner is dangerous stuff, it's better to be in some possession of your faculties before you get involved in it.

COLIN DAVIS

[Wagner's] music is like a woman: so attractive and dazzling that none of her appalling faults, hidden beneath the paint, can show.

COLIN DAVIS

Of a contralto you might say... the cellos and violas eat up her sound — cellos, viola, bassoons, clarinets, horns — very dangerous...violins...up top —no problem. ... basses and trombones...won't interfere. But this stuff thick in the middle wipes voices out.

SIR NEVILLE MARINER

He conducted with all the grace of a young elephant.

KAIKOSRU SORABJI ON THE YOUNG FURTWÄNGLER

I never use a score when conducting... Does a lion tamer enter a cage with a book on how to tame a lion?

DIMITRI MITROPOULOS

Berg's music is scarcely playable.

KARL BÖHM

Sometimes it takes excellent reflexes to follow a singer's lead — boxer's reflexes.

SIR GEORG SOLTI

We'll never forget a 1948 *Carmen* at the Prinz Regenten Theater in Munich. The orchestra's heavy non-latin rhythms and wood-chopper dynamics made it sound as if Beethoven had written it. Conductor  Solti's quasi-spastic arm movements were also a memorable distraction.

THE EDITORS

English sopranos sound as if they subsisted on sea-weed… English tenors sound like yawning giraffes.

SIR THOMAS BEECHAM

I enjoyed myself hugely, conducting, in addition to *Carmen* and *Pagliacci,* that trilogy of popular Saturday-nighters dubbed facetiously, *The English Ring — The Bohemian Girl, Maritana* and *The Lady of Killarney.*

SIR THOMAS BEECHAM

Never look at the trombones, it only encourages them.

RICHARD STRAUSS

In this profession, modesty is stupid.

LORIN MAAZEL

I have always refused to conduct opera unless conditions are absolutely right. I do it for love. No other reason.

IBID

Opera tests everything a conductor has; it begins on a level of passionate expression at which few instrumental performances ever arrive.

DAVID SCIFF

I'm often impressed by how little difference there is between well-rehearsed performances and un-rehearsed performances. It is all a question of the chemistry or atmosphere generated.

SIR CHARLES MACKERRAS

And the conductor must also formulate his views on ornamentation, unless (which is rare) he trusts his singers to decorate their own lines with skill and taste and in a consistent fashion.

MEIRION AND SUSIE HARRIES, AUTHORS OF *OPERA TODAY*

During his truncated reign in Vienna, Lorin Maazel made a practice of informing singers who failed to attend rehearsals that they were assumed to have withdrawn from the production.

RAYMOND LEPPARD

'All the Jews can go home'... When I looked in the pit all the first violinists had left it.

ZUBIN MEHTA WHEN HE DISMISSED THE CHORUS OF JEWS DURING A REHEARSAL OF *SALOME*

Something like that.

A CONDUCTOR'S GROAN AFTER A LONG, FRUSTRATING REHEARSAL, QUOTED BY GEORGETTA PSAROS

Well, he did better tonight.

THE SINGERS' KINDEST POST-PERFORMANCE COMPLIMENT ABOUT THEIR CONDUCTOR

# Is Diva Just Avid Spelled Backward?

A soprano who sang in a crowd
At the opera, had the audience wowed
When she made it quite clear
To every one's ear
If you can't make it good, make it loud

VINCENT TORRE, IN *LIMERICKS 1970-2002*

When in doubt, sing loud.

ROBERT MERRILL

My dear man, thanks to that accident in your taxi, I can sing a higher C than ever before!

FLORENCE FOSTER JENKINS PRESENTING
A BOX OF CIGARS TO A CAB DRIVER

A true lady is any amateur soprano who can sing the *Queen of the Night*'s fiery aria — but doesn't.

THE EDITORS

Hell is full of musical amateurs. Music is the brandy of the damned.

GEORGE BERNARD SHAW IN *MAN AND SUPERMAN*

Swans sing before they die
Twere no bad thing
Should certain persons
Die before they sing.

SAMUEL TAYLOR COLERIDGE

How many divas does it take to screw in a light bulb? Just one. She holds the bulb and the world revolves around her.

ANONYMOUS

This is a true diva.... Convinced of her specialness and totally uninterested in what anyone around her was doing.

MANUELA HOELTERHOFF

Zinka Milanov fan: What opera is on next Thursday?
Zinka Milanov: How would I possibly know? I'm not singing on Thursday.

JOHN GUALIANI

Leading lady soprano: What happens in the last act of *Jeremiah*?
Myron Fink composer: Haven't you read the score?
Leading lady soprano: No, why should I? I'm not in the last act.

MYRON FINK, COMPOSER

Your Brünnhilde was OK, but what fantastic horsemanship!

A FAN TO BIRGIT NILSSON WHEN HER HORSE
GRANE, MISBEHAVED ON STAGE

Renata Tebaldi... embodied the best tonal qualities and musical traditions of the purest-verismo Italian soprano, while avoiding the expressive overvehemence of her predecessors.

DAVID HAMILTON

The pain of giving oneself totally to one's art is the greatest happiness for an artist.

RENATA TEBALDI

Jeritza was gorgeous, wild and charismatic on stage, had a big voice, and knew how to use a press agent in a day when opera was still a fairly popular form.

ALBERT INNAURATO

I'm so glad she's a mezzo-soprano.

KATIA RICCIARELLI ON FIRST HEARING CECILIA BARTOLI

… Renee Fleming, perhaps the most gorgeous lyric soprano to come along since Te Kanawa and maybe even Tebaldi.

MANUELA HOELTERHOFF

La Scala is to opera what the Palace Theater was to vaudeville, what Yankee Stadium has been to baseball, what Lourdes is to people who believe in miracles.

BEVERLY SILLS

I'm the Beatles of the opera.

BEVERLY SILLS

... even in English it's hard to understand most words sung in an opera.

BEVERLY SILLS
[SO WHY NOT USE SUPERSCRIPTS FOR OPERAS IN ENGLISH?]

I felt I could do any coloratura soprano role... I always knew what I was capable of doing... in the performing arts you need ego, a certain self-assurance, or else you'd never have the guts to face an audience.

BEVERLY SILLS

45

When it comes to sheer wizardry in executing curlicues in high keys, then very few singers have matched the younger Sills.

ALBERT INNAURATO

[Beverly Sills'] *Lucia...* presents the most detailed psychological study of the part so far on record.

JOHN STEANE, *IN THE GRAND TRADITION.*

When you flop at La Scala, you don't just fall on your face, you fall down a manhole... Italians love their *pasta al dente* and their divas temperamental.

BEVERLY SILLS

La Scala may be the only opera house in the world that never has mediocre performances. La Scala has nights of glory and nights of despair. There's no in-beween.

BEVERLY SILLS [*IS LA SCALA THE ONLY PLACE?*]

The Metropolitan Opera is not a place of entertainment but a place of penance.

SIR THOMAS BEECHAM

Svetlana Serdar who got through the [*Rigoletto*] quartet... sounding like a singer rather than a hen about to lay an egg.

ELWOOD McKEE

She [Maria Callas] is the one single name in opera which is the standard by which others are measured. She is the quintessential opera singer and name.

HERBERT BRESLIN, SINGERS' AGENT

In the Reign of Rivals, of Callas and Tebaldi, singers who did impossible feats onstage were not expected to deflate into normal-size next-door neighbors when the curtain fell.

MANUELA HOELTERHOFF

Opera singers are poor, pitiful creatures; they tremble before they go onstage. Most of them come from humble backgrounds, and fame is not easily digested by someone who can barely read or write.

RUDOLF BING ON THE *DICK CAVETT SHOW*

Every singer I know can read his fee on a check and can write well enough to endorse it.

BEVERLY SILLS'S REPLY ON A LATER *DICK CAVETT SHOW*

[Rudolf] Bing and I experienced a clash of personalities. He once told a reporter: 'Not every great singer can sing at the Met'— to which I responded, 'Not every great singer wants to.'

BEVERLY SILLS, RECENTLY AND RIGHTLY CHOSEN TO HEAD THE MET

She strode on stage and the audience felt only an earthquake or a world war could keep her from going through her part.

MANUELA HOELTERHOFF

Ms. Lehmann, did you ever listen to your accent in English?

MARILYN HORNE TO LOTTE LEHMAN AFTER LOTTE REPEATEDLY PICKED ON HORNE'S GERMAN DICTION

Of a sudden, the great prima donna
Cried: 'Gawd, my voice is a gonner.'
But a cat in the wings
Said: 'I know how she sings,'
And finished the solo with honour.'
DR. LIMERICK IN *THE PENTATETTE* VOLUME XXI, NUMBER 10

During the ten years of her unquestioned reign, between 1949 and 1959, she [Callas] bestowed upon the lost souls of the world — disoriented and bewildered by the war — more music, more art, more humanity and warmth than any other individual of this century.

NOEL COWARD

Desire Defrere taught me that there are two schools of opera singing. One is concerned exclusively with making beautiful sounds... The other school features equally talented singers who... sacrifice a beautiful sound... to make a dramatic point. Maria Callas was such a singer.

BEVERLY SILLS

... [Callas] the performer who changed the standard by which all other opera singers are judged.

MICHELLE KRISEL, ARTISTIC DIRECTOR
OF THE WASHINGTON OPERA

... Callas builds her performance [in Medea] into one powerful line of ever-increasing tension. It is the kind of performance which spoils one for anything less from the opera stage.

A LONDON CRITIC

...the greatest artist of the world.

LEONARD BERNSTEIN

Everywhere I go there is chaos.

MARIA CALLAS

If you don't like the way I sing, stay home.

MARIA CALLAS

I only sign when I sing.

MARIA CALLAS BRUSHING OFF AN AUTOGRAPH HOUND

Maria gushed (to one Maria Carter in Dallas) about Onassis and his lovemaking skills. She said she wanted to give up her career and to be with him.

NICHOLAS GAGE, IN *GREEK FIRE*

A peasant on her Sunday outing.

MADAME BIKI A MILANO FASHION DESIGNER, ON HOW THE EARLY FAT 200-POUND YOUNG CALLAS DRESSED

... 25 fur coats, 40 suits, 150 pairs of shoes, 300 hats and 200 dresses.

*TIME MAGAZINE* ON CALLAS' CHIC WARDROBE IN 1956

... the greatest tragedienne since Duse.

LUCHINO VISCONTI ON MARIA CALLAS

It was impossible to tell the difference between the legs of the elephants on the stage and those of Aida sung by Maria Callas.

A CRITIC

Look, there have been many stories about this, but it's true that I ingested a tapeworm. I took it voluntarily and that's how I lost thirty kilos.

MARIA CALLAS TO GIULIETTA SIMIONATO AND QUOTED
BY NICHOLAS GAGE, IN *GREEK FIRE*

She had become another woman... conductor Carlo Maria Giulini opined, just after plump Callas had slimmed down some sixty-six pounds. She had the radiance that comes from the knowledge of beauty from within.

MADAME BIKI AFTER CALLAS THINNED
DOWN AND DRESSED WITH STYLE

Her voice, her ... sens of how music should flow, her ... rhythmic impulse, her use of tone and stress to define words and dramatic shades... To my ears was the most expressive vocal instrument ever employed in the service of music.

ROBERT RIDEOUT ON MARIA CALLAS

All divas and demi-divas with few exceptions are enchanting at a distance,... but if you would know them as near as I do, you would soon realize that they are no more real stars than those painted on any theatrical scenery; that the crowns those queens wear are only pasteboard or gilded tin, and that they are only divas or "Goddesses"... as long as their impresarios find it to their interest to pay for advertising them as such.

MAX MARETZEK, IMPRESARIO

The biographies of most divas are nearly alike, the only slight differences between them being that some, when small babies, could repeat and hum the gems of an opera at a single hearing, while others could do the same without ever having heard them, and still others could sing them before they were composed.

MAX MARETZEK

ROSA PONSELLE

... so many unforgettable hours on the stage, during which, instead of thinking of my own role, I would be lost in the dark splendor of her voice.

EZIO PINZA ON ROSA PONSELLE

# CARUSO, PAVAROTTI AND OTHER TENORS

A great singer is one with a big chest, a big mouth, ninety percent memory, ten percent intelligence, lots of hard work and something in the heart.

ENRICO CARUSO

One of the things that makes a great artist is the ability to breathe life into something that is not spontaneous but makes it appear so.

JOHN RAHBECK

**CARUSO SELF PORTRAIT**

Tenors sweat blood over it [the high-C in *Di quella pira*], develop ulcers because of it. Yet... Verdi wrote a G... a note that any tenor in any glee club is expected to be able to sing.

PLACIDO DOMINGO

The tenor with a secure top exerts a sexual fascination on people, not just women, men too. The best tenor has a quality, a timbre, that's essentially a sexual stimulant – that is why they are so highly paid.

SIR RUDOLF BING IN *THE TENORS*

Tenors get women by the score.

JAMES JOYCE PUN IN *ULYSSES*

Luciano's eye for all the pretty girls around the opera house earned him the nickname 'Passion Flower.'

GEORGE CHRISTIE, DIRECTOR THE GLYNEBOURNE FESTIVAL

To be a singer in Italy is a disgrace.

ENRICO CARUSO

Italians are skeptical of anything native, particularly tenors... anything foreign wins quick respect whether it is toothpaste or singers. It is sad that so many Italian singers must go abroad to achieve their sucess.

LUCIANO PAVAROTTI [DON'T THESE CRITERIA APPLY TO NORTH AMERICAN SINGERS TOO?]

All the time people ask me who is the singer I modeled myself after. There is no one singer. I admire different things about singers. For diction, however, my model is di Stefano.

MARIA CALLAS

Luciano Pavarotti reaches out and touches his audience in a genuine, accessible manner, engulfing his fans in waves of mutual love and passion. 'When he sings to them.' Breslin [his manager] purrs, 'he caresses them.

THE PRIVATE LIVES OF THE THREE TENORS

When Pavarotti sings, we are *all* Italian.

AN AMERICAN WRITER QUOTED IN THE PRIVATE LIVES OF THE THREE TENORS

Enrico Caruso... two hours before the performance shut himself off in his dressing room in infinite agony... At such moments the king of the tenors came down from Olympus to mix in with ordinary mortals.

ANTONA TRAVERSI

A singer can never feel he is ready. The day he assumes such a false attitude, he has stopped being a singer.

MARTTI TALVELA

The artist who boasts he is never nervous is not an artist — he is a liar or a fool.

ENRICO CARUSO

As curtain time approaches, lyric opera ceases to be an incredibly rich, tradition-laden treasure house of great art, and becomes a minefield of potential disasters

LUCIANO PAVAROTTI

... *Newsweek* on performance anxiety, cited Pavarotti as one of the most famous examples... when he (Pavarotti)... pacing nervously — found Beverly Sills chomping calmly on a bagel. "Nervous?" he asked. "Not at all" she replied. "You are lying," he said.

QUOTED IN *THE PRIVATE LIVES OF THE THREE TENORS*

I'm a fortunate man. I force myself always to incarnate the personage I'm interpreting. To be able to move the public one has to feel. The whole secret resides in the heart of the artist.

ENRICO CARUSO

He sounds like a clarinet played by an archangel.

A BELGIAN CRITIC, ABOUT ENRICO CARUSO

Your voice is the ideal which until now I have sought in vain.

FYODOR CHALIAPIN TO ENRICO CARUSO

... the most wonderful tenor I have ever heard. [His voice] rolled out like an organ... What a simple, lovable creature he was.

NELLIE MELBA, ABOUT ENRICO CARUSO

But Caruso?... He is a miracle... There will not be another Caruso for two or three hundred years... Gold swathed in velvet is his voice. He is prodigal of his power. He flings his lyrical fury over the house.

THOMAS BURKE AUTHOR, ON FIRST HEARING ENRICO CARUSO SING

Enrico Caruso, second tenor.

ENRICO CARUSO WRITING IN THE AUTOGRAPH ALBUM FILLED WITH MANY FAMOUS SINGERS' NAMES, ALL LABELED "FIRST"

No matter how much you paid him, he always turned out to be the least expensive of singers.

GIULIO GATTI-CASAZZA, MANAGER OF THE METROPOLITAN OPERA HOUSE

I have no favorite roles. I have avoided this because the moment one adopts a favorite role he becomes a specialist and ceases to be an artist.

ENRICO CARUSO

If I can draw the man who cooks my macaroni from his fire and if I can make him forget that there is such a thing as food in the world, then I know that I am touching the heights of my art.

ENRICO CARUSO

His appearance [Caruso's] was decidedly plebeian; and he was undeniably fat.

PIERRE KEY

Anyone who has traveled in Italy must have noticed the interest manifested at the opening of the opera season. This does not apply only to people with means and advanced culture, but to what might be called the general public.

ENRICO CARUSO

I am told that many people in America have the impression that my vocal ability is a kind of 'God-given gift'—that it is something which has come to me without effort. This is... absurd.

ENRICO CARUSO

... Caruso had with a remarkable vocal instrument ... it was his genius for work which made the utmost of his endowment ... and those native emotional and mental resources upon which his final artistry drew so heavily.

SALVATORE FUCITO, CARUSO'S COACH AND
ACCOMPANIST DURING HIS LAST SIX YEARS

Why don't singers stop to think? Why don't they work intelligently? Why don't they realize that all great art is a product of reserve, of restraint? Imperfect technique means imperfect art.

ENRICO CARUSO

The talent of an artist is revealed in his ability to detect and understand his shortcomings and especially in his courage to acknowledge their existence.

ENRICO CARUSO

It is sad how many people are in positions of importance in opera who don't know whether or not the singing is beautiful until they see the singer's name.

LUCIANO PAVAROTTI

I asked ART for the secret of her triumphs and she pointed to the heart, and in my artistic career, which I lived through not ingloriously, I owe to my heart my most pleasing and legitimate satisfactions. Salliano October 14, 1885

[SIGNED] ANGELO MASINI [CARUSO'S TENOR IDOL WHO BOASTED AND USED SEVEN DIFFERENT ENDINGS FOR LA DONNA È MOBILE]

Singing is like charity: You give — but you don't give everything so that you have nothing left for yourself. You have to be a little selfish.

JAN PEERCE

It is easy to perform *Il Trovatore*. All you need are the four greatest singers in the world.

ENRICO CARUSO

Pavarotti stepped to the footlights and sang all nine (high C's in *Daughter of the Regiment*) as if he were flipping pancakes into his mouth.

MANUELA HOELTERHOFF

Sopranos can be afflicted at times with odd thinking.

LUCIANO PAVAROTTI [TENORS TOO, LUCIANO. TENORS TOO!]

Don't try to think. Tenors have no brains. Everyone knows that.

KURT ADLER TO PAVAROTTI, WHO HAD SAID HE'D HAVE TO THINK ABOUT SINGING *CELESTE AIDA* AT A CONCERT THEY WERE GIVING

As for Caruso, there are no comparisons... To me, Caruso is rightly the tenor against whom all the rest of us are measured.

LUCIANO PAVAROTTI

Luciano has a way of making each person in the audience... feel that he is singing directly to them. He sets up the most intensely personal lines of communication. It is extraordinary.

JOHN WUSTMAN, PAVAROTTI'S ACCOMPANIST

Pavarotti is not just the greatest tenor since Caruso, he is the greatest tenor ever.

HERBERT VON KARAJAN [1973]

By holding the white handkerchief, I keep myself in one spot. If I were to start making large gestures, the handkerchief would fly all over the place and catch my attention like a warning flag... It is my security blanket while on the concert stage.

LUCIAON PAVAROTTI

Audiences tend to be the same everywhere.... If I am in good form, they respond well, if I am in less good form, they respond less well. I never blame an audience if they are not enthusiastic.

LUCIANO PAVAROTTI

If you put together the voices and talents of Gigli, Pertile, Martinelli, Lauri-Volpi, Schipa, and the rest, their combination still wouldn't be fit to kiss Enrico Caruso's shoes.

GIOVANNI MARTINELLI, TENOR

What if Caruso is remembered as a clown whose antics extended down to the point of his pencil as a cartoonist? He was the clown whose heart is breaking, that leaps through the circus hoop into the heart of man.

MARY ELLIS PELTZ

A group of reporters once asked Caruso what he thought of Babe Ruth. Caruso, who was unfailingly polite and amiable, replied that he didn't know because unfortunately he had never heard her sing.

*BARTLETT'S FAMILIAR ANECDOTES*

In the program for the *Ballo in Maschera* performance (at the Philadelphia Academy of Music) EMI proclaimed Corelli the greatest tenor in the world. Di Stefano demanded that the programs be collected and the page ripped out.

D. STEIN (INTERNET)

Don't forget: before you drink the love potion, you're a baritone. After that, you're a tenor.

GUSTAV MAHLER, CONDUCTOR AND COMPOSER
TO THE TENOR SINGING TRISTAN

In his tenth-floor New York apartment composer and author Deems Taylor and his guest from Ireland, the tenor John McCormack, were jovially chatting away when a loud collision on the street below made them dash to the window. Peering down, they saw a large truck had slammed into the rear of another truck, its exact twin. In a tone of mock surprise, McCormack announced, "I didn't know it was their mating season."

JOHN GUALIANI

... Giovanni Martinelli, asked by a reporter why he had endorsed a certain brand of cigarettes, declaring they didn't irritate his throat. "Yes, yes, of course I gave that endorsement. How could they irritate my throat? I have never smoked."

*BARTLETT'S FAMILIAR ANECDOTES*

The one thing I hate at the Met is the note in the program that the public is requested not to interrupt the music with applause. That should be destroyed. What we need is to be encouraged to applaud.

PLACIDO DOMINGO

When I sang Pinkerton I took good care to promote myself to commander in the third act.

JOHN MCCORMACK

About a really ideal production of *Tristan* the tenor [Jess Thomas] says he can imagine it any number of ways — he'd even be willing to play Act Two in the nude, given the right director, circumstances and, no doubt, the right Isolde.

ROBERT JACOBSON WRITING ABOUT JESS THOMAS, HELDENTENOR

The *Götterdämmerung* Siegfried is a very interesting personality; however, I refused to sing the young Siegfried, because I think he is a bore. I always call him a Wagnerian L'il Abner.

JON VICKERS

Any competent artist will be more interesting to listen to at forty-five than at twenty-five.

PLACIDO DOMINGO

I don't want to be a slave. Nobody ... on the grand opera stage is anything else. When I want to sing, I sing. When I don't ... I don't . The grand opera tenor — he sings when he's told.

TONY PONZILLO (ROSA PONSELLE'S TENOR BROTHER)

One fart from Caruso would drown out all the tenors on stage today.

[IN ITALIAN: UNA SCORREGGIA DI CARUSO MANGEREBBE<br>TUTTI IN TENORI OGGI IN ARTE] TITTA RUFFO

If one day I arrive at a routine — the day that going to the stage becomes like going to the office — then I'll seriously consider stopping. For me, to perform must be the most exciting point in my life — every time.

JOSE CARRERAS

An evening never recovers from a cracked high note. It is exactly like a bullfight. You are not allowed one mistake.

LUCIANO PAVAROTTI

He had no right... to positively refuse singing at the side of an excellent and most estimable artist, whom, with a purblind insolence only to be found in Italian vocalists, he believed not equal to his own degree of merit.

MAX MARETZEK ON BENEDETTI, 19TH CENTURY TENOR

Director Lofti Mansouri: What's the matter, Franco?
Tenor Franco Bonisolli: (pacing around backstage in a
         daze) Pavarotti and Domingo are out to get me!"
Director Lofti Mansouri: Franco, Pavarotti and
         Domingo don't even know who you are.

LOFTI MANSOURI

# BARITONES AND BASSES HAVE MORE TESTOSTERONE

TITTA RUFFO

Basses in opera are good only as cuckold husbands, priests and doges. The baritones are the real lovers, the real Don Giovannis.

ARTURO TOSCANINI TO BARITONE PAOLO SILVERI

Titta Ruffo… one of the greatest dramatic baritones of the 20th century.

JEAN-PIERRE MOUCHON IN *THE RECORD COLLECTOR* VOL. 37, 1998

I have known only three vocal miracles: Caruso, Ponselle and Ruffo.

TULLIO SERAFIN, CONDUCTOR

But that was not a voice, that was a miracle.

GIUSEPPE DE LUCA ON RUFFO'S VOICE

… alterations in the laryngeal cavity… permitted Ruffo to reach intensities never attained by heroic baritones such as Antonio Magini-Coletti, Domenico Viglione-Borghese, Jean Noté, or, more recently, Gino Bechi, Ettore Bastianini, Leonard Warren, Cornell MacNeil and Sherrill Milnes.

JEAN-PIERRE MOUCHON

Ruffo delights in the introspective or in climaxes sounding like erupting volcanoes. With chameleon-like changes… colourful, unctuous, elastic, supple, ingratiating, fiendish, colourless, white or tortured… supported by an uncanny breath-control.

IBID

The characteristics of Ruffo… a resonant voice, a magnificent power in the middle and upper registers and a superb palette which beggars description… darkness, brilliance and strength…

IBID

King of the Baritones.

ONE OF RUFFO'S NICKNAMES

Titta Ruffo… sang in line with the tastes of those days.
IBID [COMMENT: TASTES HAVE CHANGED A BIT]

I sang too much for the gallery and that wore my voice down and shortened my career.
TITTA RUFFO TO THE EDITOR [HIS CAREER: 1898-1936]

I have never given a singing lesson. I have given advice on interpretation of various roles. I don't know how I managed to sing, so how can I dare teach others something I don't understand myself. The only technical advice I can give you, Stefano, or any one else is sing in the "maschera" and always let your lower jaw hang down loosely like a limp prick.
IBID

FIGARO & MEPHISTOPHELES COSTUMES

With the possible exception of Ezio Pinza, no one worked harder at a Casanova image than Fyodor Chaliapin.
ROSA PONSELLE, SOPRANO

Chaliapin, in fine fettle, told me that he had shared his bed the night before with a nice young gal and in the morning he had offered her two tickets to the opera that night, but she had looked down sadly and said she could not accept his kind offer because she and her family had no proper clothes to go to the opera. "We are so poor we need money just to buy bread," she added. "Well, if you need-

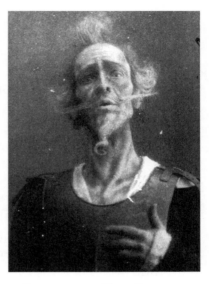

CHALIAPIN AS DON QUICHOTTE

ed bread, you should have spent the night with a baker," Chaliapin replied.

TITTA RUFFO, AS TOLD TO THE EDTITOR

Chaliapin and I were close pals. We both had strong views on life, laughter, music, interpretation, costuming and make-up and our views were close, but not always the same. He was more of a broad-natured bohemian than I. Once in Monte Carlo, he was feeling very expansive and said, "Ruffochki, you must come to my birthday party." When I arrived I saw every one around the huge table were women and children, his women and his children. I was the only outsider. Chaliapin introduced me and said, "these are my wonderful wives and children."

There must have been some sixteen women there. Every one was in a gay, friendly mood and Chaliapin went around the table hugging, kissing, toasting and making sure all vodka glasses were refilled again and again.

It was indeed a great, laid-back and unusual birthday party, but then Fyodor was an unusual man.

TITTA RUFFO, AS TOLD TO THE EDTITOR

There are only three kinds of opera singers: those who cannot act at all; those who imitate and copy; and those who try to create according to their own conceptions. Only the latter deserve to be called artists.

EZIO PINZA

What impressed me most was the intelligence with which he [Chaliapin] limited his  movements and gestures to psychological necessity.  They were very sparing, but when he moved, the whole stage shifted with him.

EZIO PINZA

In Chicago, Fyodor Chaliapin was singing Boris Godunov. He thought almost none of the listeners knew Russian, so he ad libbed to his man servant in the wings, "Get the whiskey bottle out; this opera's almost over."

FROM OPERA ANTICS & ANECDOTES

A bronze Roman god come to life
Ezio the magnificent
Don Juan of the Metropolitan
One of the fourteen most glamorous men in the world

NEWSPAPER CLIPPINGS ABOUT EZIO PINZA

Pinza's voice is so masculine, they say hairs grow on his vocal cords!

THE EDITOR

What he [Pinza] did was what made the Golden Age golden. He was an actor who could sing, a singer who could act.

IRVING KOLODIN, CRITIC

EZIO PINZA

One felt glad to be alive in Pinza's time... The gods were good to Pinza. They gave him a magnificent throat, fine appearance, dramatic flair, and rare intelligence — qualities which, in combination made for a top operatic artist.

ROBERT LAWRENCE, CRITIC

... he [Toscanini] taught me most of what I know about style in operatic singing.

EZIO PINZA

... Maestro Tullio Serafin, one of the finest opera conductors I have ever worked with.

EZIO PINZA

But in *Don Giovanni* there is a truly monumental discrepancy between the build-up of the hero as a romantic figure, an irresistible, heartless, dashing seducer — and the failures of his attempted conquests on the stage.

EZIO PINZA

Beautiful women found handsome Pinza irrestible —
and vice versa. Outside their home, Mrs. Augusta Pinza
was afraid to let him out of her sight for more than ten
minutes. Was Pinza as Don Giovanni flagrant type cast-
ing? Well, his first *Don Giovanni* at the Met was
panned by the critic of the New York Herald Tribune.
Pinza grew into the role and made his own, probably
with some helpful guidance from mentors such as
Bruno Walter, Toscanini and Serafin. Most singers, and,
notoriously, Italians need special training to do Mozart
right.

THE EDITORS

## BURMA SHAVING CREAM ADS

I'm Onegin
You're allset!
But with his whiskers
She said, "Nyet!"
BURMA SHAVE

The greatest basso
Can't be wooly
Must cut beard
To sing out fully
BURMA SHAVE

In a *Rigoletto* produced by Boris Goldovsky, young
Sherrill Milnes was singing the title role in English.
Nearing the end of Rigoletto's monologue, *Pari siamo*,
instead of, "it is an evil omen; ah, no, it's madness,"
Sherrill sang, "It is an oval eeman." Then realizing his
fluff, he ad libbed, "ah, no! It's a round one."

AN AUDIENCE MEMBER

# Sex and Opera

Why is everyone so interested in sex and its effect on the voice? Maybe it's because singers have always looked for excuses when they are not in voice and too much lovemaking is a noble excuse.

Luciano Pavarotti

I think sex tunes the body the way vocalizing tunes the voice. I vocalize every day.

Luciano Pavarotti, from a *Newsweek* interview

You can sing badly five minutes afterward (after sex) and you can sing badly five days afterward. I do not think the connection is so definite as many would have you believe.

Luciano Pavarotti

I do believe that high notes can be temporarily affected by sexual intercourse a night or even two or three nights before a performance. Singers can't afford to overdo sex.

Jan Peerce in *The Bluebird of Happiness*

Denying sex does not make you sing well.

Jan Peerce

My husband won't have sex with me for three nights before he sings and is too tired to have it for three nights afterwards. Since he's singing every fourth night, I want you to know that you have ruined our sex life.

Mrs. Franco Corelli to Rudolf Bing

Maestro Orgasmo.

Gaetano Donizetti's nickname quoted by Basil Howitt

Basso Ezio Flagello was seated on a train between the wives of two famous tenors.
"How long has it been for you?" "Three months." "How long for you?" "Four months."
Flagello said, "If I can be of service to either of you ladies?"

QUOTED BY TONY RANDALL IN *WHICH REMINDS ME*

Tenor Student: Maestro, how many days before a performance must a tenor do without sex?
Tenor & teacher Jean de Reszke: Oh, maybe two days or so.
Tenor Student: What about sopranos?
Jean de Reszke: Well, at least they shouldn't do it on stage.

JOHN GUALIANI

Believe me, I come to New York for three things: music, money and men.

LJUBA WELITSCH

Luciano's eye for all the pretty girls around the opera house earned him the nickname 'Passion Flower.'

GEORGE CHRISTIE, OF THE GLYNEBOURNE FESTIVAL OPERA

Sex is good for my voice, but I can't speak for all tenors. I am never in bed with a tenor.

JOSE CARRERAS

All my wenches now pass before my eyes.

RICHARD WAGNER, TO HIS SECOND WIFE COSIMA, SHORTLY BEFORE HIS DEATH. QUOTED IN *LOVE LIVES OF THE GREAT COMPOSERS*

Same sex desire.

ABOUT GEORGE FRIDERIC HANDEL, QUOTED IN *MORE LOVE LIVES OF THE GREAT COMOSERS* BY BASIL HOWITT

I look for sentiment as well as sex.

Vincenzo Bellini

… a base soul who went about pouring a kind of bath water melody down the back of every woman he met.

George Moore, Irish novelist, about Charles Gounod

The philandering monk

Basil Howitt, describing Charles Gounod

Orgies with Arab boys and fellaheen

Basil Howitt, about Camille Saint-Saëns

His susceptibility to [his mother-in-law's] charm seems to have been quite as real and strong as his love for his wife.

About Georges Bizet, in *Bizet and His World* by Mina Curtiss

Bewitching in music, bastard in love.

Basil Howitt about Claude Debussy

Luigi Ricci (1805-1859) was prolific not just as a composer of comic operas.He was also famous thanks to the beautiful Bohemian twin sopranos who became his mistresses. He claimed they looked so much alike he could not tell them apart. This was probably true: he had four children by one and  five by the other. There is more than one theory why Luigi went insane and died so young.

The Editors, from Opera Antics & Anecdotes

# How to Sing

A singer able to sing so much as sixteen bars of good music in a natural, well-poised and sympathetic voice, without effort, without affectation, without tricks, without exaggeration, without hiatuses, without hiccupping, without barking, without baa-ing. Such a singers is very rare, an excessively rare bird.

HECTOR BERLIOZ

It's not always the voice... It's emotional security, intelligence, chance. Careers are determined by so many factors... I've seen people's careers harmed by emotional difficulties, wrong repertoire choices, and schedules that were too unchallenging and kept them from growing artistically.

MATTHEW EPSTEIN, SINGERS' MANAGER

[Beniamino] Gigli had a very unique style which he enhanced by his use of sobs. He used them as a means of expression but above all to relax himself, to rest his voice.

RENATA TEBALDI

There are as many techniques as there are singers, since each student, while possibly adhering to his teacher's guidance, finds usually through trial and error things that work for them, things that don't.

G. PAUL PADILLO

Student: Maestro, do you advocate pear-shaped tones?
Teacher: It depends.
Student: What do you mean?
Teacher: It depends which end of the pear you hear first.

ORVILLE WHITE, VOICE TEACHER

72

Always save a little breath for your final note — the tenor will do the same.
MARIA CALLAS, GIVING ADVICE AT A MASTER CLASS

When you go for a high note, think of stinking fish.
ANONYMOUS

Beegah mout', beegah voice. Mout' like-ah fish, Naut-uh puckered like chicken derriere.
BERNARDO DE MURO, DRAMATIC TENOR & VOICE TEACHER

Singing teachers say you must never open your mouth in the wind, which, I think, is a superstition.
LAWRENCE TIBBETT, IN *THE GLORY ROAD*

Opera Buff: Who would you say is a good voice teacher in New York?
Met General Manager Giulio Gatti-Casazza: A good voice teacher is one who is lucky enough to find a pupil with a great natural voice — and doesn't ruin it.
ORVILLE WHITE, VOICE TEACHER

Quite a few voice coaches learned how to teach technique while working as accompanists for singers or as studio pianists for other voice teachers.
THE EDITORS

Many very fine singing teachers were never singers at all or didn't have good enough voices to become famous. [You don't have to be a chicken to cook an omelet]
JOHN CARGHER

When a singer runs into vocal problems he cannot correct, he thinks he's now competent to teach others.

MAESTRO ARTURO MERLINI, FORMER
HEAD VOICE COACH AT LA SCALA

Just anyone, with or without actual professional experience can teach without certification... Does this leave the field open to charlatans?

JAMES CALVERT

No amount of personality projection makes up for vocal trouble.

SIR RUDOLF BING

I think one of the best exercises for learning to control the voice... is to stand erect... and slowly sniff in air through the nostrils, inhaling in little puffs, as if you were smelling something.

LUISA TETRAZZINI, COLORATURA SOPRANO

You may have been accustomed for years to take a note in a certain way, and after a long while you discover that, while it is a very good way, there is a better one.

LUISA TETRAZZINI

I teach *bel canto.* Every one else teaches *can belto.*

JOHN GUALIANI

Voice Student: How should one inhale before the first note in a phrase?
Tenor Fernando De Lucia: My son, I know only one way: *breathe*!

JOHN GUALIANI

I've taught you all I know — and you know NOTHING!
AN ANONYMOUS VOICE TEACHER TO HIS STUDENT,
ACCORDING TO ORVILLE WHITE

Sing on your interest, not on your capital.
AN OLD APOCRYPHAL CHESTNUT

True interpretation occurs when not one single note of the original remains.
ALDO REGGIOLI, BASSO AND SINGING TEACHER

If you push and try to force out a sound that is bigger than what naturally belongs to the voice, you have a problem. Many tenors have trouble because of this.
LUCIANO PAVAROTTI

We have a saying in this business: the student makes the teacher famous. The top teachers all have one famous artist — never two.
GUISEPPE DI STEFANO [MANUEL GARCIA, MATILDE MARCHESI,
ANTONIO COTOGNI ETC HAD MANY, GIUSEPPE]

Madness seems to improve the art of singing.
ALBERT EINSTEIN

# National Tastes and Distastes

They say opera in Finland is dead. That's ridiculous!
You can't die before you're born.

MARTTI TALVELA'S COMMENT TO THE EDITORS IN THE 1960s

Mario del Monaco joked how hard it was to satisfy
acting tastes in every country where he sang. In *Otello*,
for instance, he had to act three different death scenes,
depending on where he was.

"In Italy, I stab myself, stumble around, sink to the floor
and then, with superhuman effort, I struggle up onto
the bed, kiss Desdemona and slither slowly down for
the long count. Now, in New York that won't do. In
America when you're down, you're down, and you
don't get up. So in America I stab myself, fall on the
bed and later sink slowly to the floor on Otello's final
notes. But at the Colon in Buenos Aires, where they
pay me twice as much as I get in New York or Italy — I
die twice."

MARIO DEL MONACO TO THE EDITOR,
FROM *OPERA ANTICS & ANECDOTES*

... Italians are charming — am I not Italian myself? But
they are slow, happy-go-lucky... It's not easy to bawl
them out... they look at you with such hurt eyes... you
want to embrace them and apologize for your rude-
ness.

GIAN CARLO MENOTTI, IN *A LITTLE NIGHT MUSIC*

Italian audiences know exactly what they want in opera
and, depending on what they get, lift you to the skies
with their rapture or crush you to the ground with
derision.

EZIO PINZA IN *OPERA ANTICS & ANECDOTES*

I believe from the bottom of my heart that, inherently and permanently, the English are an unmusical people. They do not like fire, nor passion, nor great moments in either life or art. Mozart's music, that runs peacefully and simply along, is precisely what suits them best. They adore it. They likewise adore Rossini and Handel. They think that the crashing emotional climaxes of the more advanced composers are extravagant; and, both by instinct and principle, they dislike the immoderate and the extreme in all things. They are in fact a simple and primitive people, temperamentally, actually, and artistically.

CLARA LOUISE KELLOGG IN
*MEMOIRS OF AN AMERICAN PRIMA DONNA*

German audiences dislike loud, blaring opera singing, unless the opera is by Wagner.

A FOREIGN OBSERVER

In Germany before World War II, Italian and French operas were sung in German, whereas now many are sung in the original language. In America, it's just the other way round: before the war, operas were almost all in the original language, but now many are given in English.

THE EDITORS

I said, "Look, I can't do this in English, but we have a cast that doesn't speak German, and 90% of the audience won't understand German, so what are we to do?"

ZUBIN MEHTA CONDUCTOR, ON A PRODUCTION OF *DIE FLEDERMAUS*

Why is the Colon theater in Argentina named after a part of the digestive tract?

ANONYMOUS

# PLOYS TO LAND CONTRACTS

If you can imitate your rival's voice perfectly, call up the General Manager, say you are unfortunately ill and unable to sing tonight. Then still in your rival's voice, recommend yourself as the ideal substitute.

JOHN GUALIANI

A young Italian singer I knew could mimic perfectly the voice of Italian Prime Minister Mario Scelba. So, he had his girl friend call up the General Manager's office at the Rome Opera and explain that Prime Minister Scelba was on the line. Then he purred into the General Manager's ear in Scelba's voice, 'My dear fellow, why don't you sign up that wonderful young opera singer So-and-So? He'll be at your office at 10:00 tomorrow morning. I shall not forget your kindness in this matter.' A contract, of course, awaited my young pal's signature. I and his other buddies wondered how the hell he'd managed to land such a contract. One evening over wine, he laughingly confessed the caper — privately.

JOHN GUALIANI

If you are going to sing five performances, offer to sing one as a benefit for the Artistic Director. He gets your fee. That way you are much more likely to be invited back to sing again.

SOPRANO LYNNE STROW

Lillian Norton of Maine and Arthur Scovell of Detroit were studying voice in 1879 with the same Maestro in Milan. He had them change their names to Lilliana Nordica and Auturo Scovelli and arranged for them to debut together in *Traviata* in Brescia. A goodly sum of under-the-table money calmed the Brescia opera's qualms about engaging not *one* but *two* foreigners, and *Americans* at that... Nordica, for the party scenes, wore a pearl necklace loaned to her by President Teddy Roosevelt's cousin, Cornelia who happened to be Scovell's wife. Studying opera singing in Europe was very *chique* for upper crust Americans before radio and the talkie movies came along.

JOHN GUALIANI

Though in many cities this does not work, have your husband or some one else pass discreetly, via an intermediary if necessary, a tidy sum of money to some key decision maker, such as the General Manager or Artistic Director.

ANONYMOUS

Get under a good conductor.

ANONYMOUS

Going to bed with me gives you no hope for a better part. Understand that? *No hope.* But if you don't go to bed with me, you have the *certainty* of no better part.

LA SCALA GENERAL MANAGER ANTONIO GHIRINGHELLI TO<br>MARIA CALLAS, FROM *MARIA CALLAS THE WOMAN BEHIND*<br>*THE LEGEND* BY ARIANNA STASSINOPOULOS

Marry the General Manager, Artistic Director, or the major *angel* who donates more money to the company than any one else.

THE EDITORS

You've got to be prepared to be the victim of luck. It's not the notices often that make the difference but meeting people. You've got to be ready to take the opportunities.

BRYAN DRAKE

79

# Audience Twits and Twaddle

Fan: My dear, you have never sung better!
Elderly Nellie Melba: Oh, but, my dear friend, I have.

APOCRYPHAL

I always wanted to just take a bow at the end of an act in which I had not yet appeared onstage to upset the audience into thinking, "Who is that? How did we miss *him*?"

DAVID GEARY, IN *SINGERS OF TODAY*

I accept their criticism and jeers only on the condition that I do not have to be grateful for their applause.

GIUSEPPE VERDI, ON AUDIENCES

She: That tenor you like is earning lots of kudos in
       Europe.
He: You got it wrong, honey. They're called euros,
     not kudos.

THE EDITORS OF *GLOBAL TRAVEL LAUGHS*

I've been reading in the paper that it [Berg's *Lulu*] was written in the twelve tone row. No wonder I didn't enjoy it. I was sitting in the sixteenth row.

H. E. DICKSON, IN *GENTLEMEN, MORE DOLCE PLEASE*

Boston audiences aren't very big, but make up in coldness for their sparse numbers.

GERALDINE FARRAR, WARNING ENRICO CARUSO

[Season-subscription boxes] separated the cream of society from the milk and whey.

ANONYMOUS

Well, at least now we don't have to feel sorry for Madam Butterfly.

ATTRIBUTED TO AN OLD-LINE BOSTONIAN
DOWAGER JUST AFTER PEARL HARBOR

Bel canto is gone.
Where did she go?
Where did *who* go?
Belle Canto.

FROM *OPERA ANTICS & ANECDOTES*

What difference does it make whether they sing in English or in the original language? Either way, you can't understand the words they are singing.

MRS. JESS WALTERS

I do not mind what language an opera is sung in as long as I do not understand it.

EDWARD APPLETON

There is... hostility in any audience, even if they're your friends... If you give a great performance, they'll be the first to cheer... But they also come like aficionados to a bullfight: to see the giant fall, the matador gored... Friends!

JAN PEERCE

I found the theatre full of people talking in normal voices, their backs to the stage. The singers, undeterred, gesticulated and yelled their lungs out... People were gambling, eating supper in their boxes, etc.

HECTOR BERLIOZ, ON A PERFORMANCE IN
ITALY OF *L'ELISIR D'AMORE*

I love Beethoven, specially the poems.

RINGO STARR

81

My Aunt Sally was so dumb, she asked if *opera buffa* meant opera in the buff, nude. Also, in the foyer when she overheard some one talking about *do wop music,* she was shocked and thought the speaker was making a racial slur and suggesting that Italian music be performed.

THE EDITORS

Habitués of the Metropolitan Opera House have been called upon to suffer many things to compensate for the privilege of listening to their great singers — incompetent and inane stage management, miserable and inappropriate scenery and costumes, a chorus wretched in vocal equipment and squalid in appearance.

RICHARD ALDRICH, *TIMES* CRITIC IN 1900

A VERSATILE PROMPTER ENJOYING HIS WORK

# PUTDOWNS AND SNIDE REMARKS

The ensemble sounded like feeding time at the zoo.

*APOCRYPHAL*

The trouble with a lot of songs you hear nowadays is that somebody forgot to put them to music.

*SAMMY KAHN*

… the size of the brain is often in inverse ratio to the size of the voice.

*JOHN CARGHER*

The higher the voice the smaller the intellect.

*ERNEST NEWMAN*

She had no problem with head voice or chest voice, but there is no clear evidence of a brain.

*A CRITIC*

If she had in her lower register what she's lacking in her top, she'd have a good middle.

*JOHN GUALIANI*

The best voices don't live in the larynx of the singer or the diaphragm, but in the (often empty) space between the ears.

*APOCRYPHAL*

If a singer has any brains, they are (pointing to his own throat) here.

*ARTURO TOSCANINI DURING WORLD WAR II UPON LEARNING THAT, EZIO PINZA HAD JUST SPENT THE NIGHT IN A BOSTON JAIL FOR MAKING PRO-MUSSOLINI REMARKS*

.... pint-sized Francisco Araiza. When he stood next to the ample Amelia of the evening, Deborah Voigt, it looked as if she were ventriloquizing with a hand puppet.

MANUELA HOELTERHOFF

... singers, whose talent is often not related to any sort of educational culture.

JONATHAN MILLER, OPERA PRODUCER

Domingo would have to go pray in seventeen churches in Guadalajara to find that (Pavarotti's) sound.

HERBERT BRESLIN, PAVAROTTI'S AGENT

My top went thin and my squillo went raw
So Pav, Jose, and I pulled off a *cute ménàge-a-trois*
But I'll keep getting claps and raking in big dough
So long as I keep trilling in '*O Sole Mio.*'

DENNIS RYAN IN *THE BALLAD OF PLACIDO DOMINGO*

... Mario del Monaco, who had a voice so big he could fit Domingo into a tooth cavity.

CHRISTOPHER RAEBURN, RECORDING EXECUTIVE

Tenor Luciano Pavarotti
Tried high notes 'cause he was naughty.
Cracked one good, but not in Parma.
Otherwise he'd have bought the farm-a.

FROM *PENTATETTE*, THE LIMERICK PERIODICAL

My dear, best be careful! Your high C is sounding a little low tonight.

ANGELA GHEORGHIU, TO A RIVAL SOPRANO

Her voice sounded like an eagle being goosed.

RALPH NOVAK

Have him come in, but tell him to leave his C-sharp on the coat-rack. He can pick it up on his way out.

GIOACCHINO ROSSINI ABOUT HIS VISITOR,
TENOR GILBERT-LOUIS DUPREZ

Working with you has been the most hideous experience of my life, and I will never do it again.

CAROL VANESS TO KATHLEEN BATTLE AFTER THE FINAL
CURTAIN OF *THE MARRIAGE OF FIGARO*

If you want to make the best possible impression, just lip synch the part and I'll sing it for you behind stage.

A SOPRANO TO HER RIVAL

The day... Renata Tebaldi sings *Norma* or *Lucia* or *Anna Bolena* one night and *La Traviata, La Gioconda,* or *Medea* the next, then and only then will I consider her a rival. Otherwise, it would be like comparing champagne... Coca Cola.

MARIA CALLAS

Rossini:      I feel very depressed.
Meyerbeer: You've been listening to too much of your
              own music.

Cannot go to Cleveland. Have tenor rabies.

BIRGIT NILSSON IN A WIRE TO RUDOLF BING, AFTER
CORELLI ALLEGEDLY BIT HER NECK IN *TURANDOT*
[CORELLI CLAIMED THIS WAS "A GOOD STORY," BUT UNTRUE]

Some musicologists see Wotan as representing the absent father figure who Wagner longed for in his own life. Far too Freudian and weird to think about — a topic best avoided altogether.

DAVID BARBER

Ah, I see Pippers is in the shit again!
EILEEN FARRELL, REFERRING TO CONDUCTOR THOMAS SCHIPPERS

A vile beastly rottenheaded foolbegotten brazen-throated pernicious piggish screaming, tearing, roaring, perplexing. splitmecrackle, cashmecriggle insane ass of a woman is practizing howling below-stairs with a brute of a singing master so horrible that my head is nearly off.
EDWARD LEAR IN A LETTER TO LADY STRACHEY IN 1859

## What is this? Great Self-confidence or Shameless Vanity

Relax! When you're singing with me, Mary, you're in the big time!

RICHARD TUCKER, IN AN ASIDE TO MARIA CALLAS
DURING A *TOSCA* PERFORMANCE

Lucky girl!

MRS. RICHARD TUCKER TO MARTINA ARROYO WHO
ANNOUNCED SHE WAS TO SING WITH RICHARD

... the characteristics of a successful virtuoso: self-indulgent, self-dedicated and a hero of all your dreams.

OSCAR LEVANT

I'm no more humble than my talents require.

OSCAR LEVANT

With each artist — you never know what little sack of encouragements they carry around with them. I suppose the so-called faith in ourselves is the foundation of our talent, but sure these encouragements are the mortar that holds it together.

PAVAROTTI: *MY OWN STORY WITH WILLIAM WRIGHT*

The only thing I am proud about is that I'm not proud.

KARL KIENLECHNER, BARITONE AND VOICE COACH IN MUNICH

Let's not talk about me. Let's talk about you. What do *you* think of *me*?

ALBERT SCHMIDT, QUOTED IN *OPERA ANTICS & ANECDOTES*

To Pietro Mascagni with highest esteem and immutable affection {signed} Pietro Mascagni.

PIETRO MASCAGNI, DEDICATING A COPY OF<br>
LE MASCHERE TO HIMSELF

### Mother of the Famous Composer

GIOACCHINO ROSSINI, HIS WAY OF<br>
ADDRESSING HIS MOTHER IN LETTERS

I think a lot of Leonard Bernstein — but not as much as he does.

OSCAR LEVANT

I wonder if George Gershwin had to do it all over, would he fall in love with himself again?

OSCAR LEVANT

A DIVA WRITES HER MEMOIRS

# A WOULD HAVE-BEEN PRIMA DONNA
## REMINISCENCES

When I was fifteen I starred in an Oshkosh High production of *Oklahoma.* Our music teacher, some family friends, and the local music critic said I had just the right voice for opera. "Wow!" I thought, "maybe there's more money in country western or musical comedy, but I'll just take me a couple of voice lessons, sign on with a good agent and next year I'll be at the footlights at the Met, picking up all those flowers my fans will toss me. Hi-diddly-dee a diva's life for me! — That was fifty years ago.

My voice coach in Wisconsin, Madam Fedora Zilchkovich, brought me a slight step closer to reality. "When you are ready, my dear, in two or three years, I'll send a letter to old Professor Dingelmauser in Germany and he will arrange proper auditions and introductions for you in both Germany and Austria."

Five years and thousands of vocalises and dollars later, I was still certain I would be America's next Rise Stevens. So, I took a lonely trip and auditioned at several lower-tier theaters in Germany and Austria.

In Europe I learned there were only two openings in all of Germany and Austria for mezzos in my repertory or Fach. (Why hadn't Madam Zilchkovich back in Wisconsin known this and told me?) Furthermore, over two hundred singers from all corners of the planet were vying for those two spots.

Back in Wisconsin and very glum, I contemplated a life as a music teacher. European friends I had made during the auditions wrote and said the singers who landed those two contracts had run-of-the-mill voices, but top-of-the-line connections — and, as one German soprano wrote me, "connections hurt only those who have none."

Looking back, I now know that any singers who attained star billing most often got their first important contract through some one with clout, a door-opener whose recommendation could not be disregarded by local opera bigwigs. "Give this young mezzo a chance or I'll cash in all my bonds and never give your damned opera another cent!" That approach gets far more attention than a beautiful voice or winning a voice competition.

I had a fine voice and I was thin enough to play heroine or even pants roles, such as Octavian and Cherubino, but I found that without that someone with leverage to open a door for me, launching a career was a do-it-yourself kit that came with the zipper stuck.

So now I say to young singers to look hard for door-openers, cultivate them, and be nice to them. Otherwise,you'll end up like me: teaching music, singing now and then in church and warbling at the Tuesday Morning Music Club.

# CRITICS SKEWER COMPOSERS, PERFORMERS AND PERFORMANCES

Don't pay any attention to critics. Don't even ignore them.

SAMUEL GOLDWYN, HOLLYWOOD FILM PRODUCER

No, no, and thrice no! The German people have nothing in common with this open public scandal

LUDWIG SPEIDEL, AFTER THE WORLD PREMIERE OF *TÄNNHAUSER*

Unnecessary... immoral and unspeakably degrading... so revolting, indecent and impure that it ought never to have been tolerated on the English stage.

THE CRITIC OF *THE ERA* COMMENTS ON THE INCEST THEME IN WAGNER'S *RING* (1882)

*Wozzeck* is the work of a Chinaman from Vienna.

QUOTED BY GIGLIOLA GALLI

*Manon Lescaut* is sentimentality at its thickest and greasiest.

ERNEST NEWMAN

Pornophony.

AN AMERICAN CRITIC ON *LADY MACBETH OF MTSENSK*

[She] launched into a rendition of *Un bel dì* [in English] that sounded like two wet cats tied into a pillowcase and being stepped on.

G. PAUL PADILLO

A critic is a man who knows the way, but can't drive the car.

KENNETH TYNAN

A famous critic came to call on Verdi just as the great composer was finishing up his opera *Il Trovatore.* Verdi sat down at the piano and played some of the music from the opera. "What do you think?" he asked.

"That's terrible," the critic replied.

"Well, what about this?" Verdi asked, playing another number.

"That's even worse!" shuddered the critic.

"All right, just one more…" And Verdi played the "Anvil Chorus."

"Oh, my goodness! Absolutely horrible!" cried the critic, covering his ears.

Verdi, smiling broadly, got up from the piano and threw his arms around the critic. "Oh, thank you so much!" he cried, "I've been writing an opera for the common people of Italy. If you, the eminent and refined critic, had liked it, then nobody else would have. But if you hate it, that means the whole world will love it!"

PRINTED IN *OPERA FOR DUMMIES*
BY SCOTT SPECK AND DAVID POGUE

Music critics are an unnecessary evil. They serve no useful purpose… Many don't know anything about music and those who know a great deal  about it have no feeling for it. They go… to criticize, not to enjoy.

JEROME TOOBIN IN *AGITATO*

Having the critics praise you is like having the hangman say you've got a pretty neck.

ELI WALLACH

[A critic is] a virgin who wants to teach Don Juan how to make love.

TRISTAN BERNARD, IN *STRIKING BACK AT CRITICS*

Oblivion and neglect are the worst fate that can befall a composition, especially a new one. It is not so much meaningful what the critic writes; that he should write something is the important matter.

PYOTR TCHAIKOVSKY

The funny thing is that even if I know someone has written a bad review about me, I am not upset unless I read it. But I need a great deal of self-discipline not to read the review, as I am always curious to know what has been written.

SIR GEORG SOLTI, IN HIS *MEMOIRS*

Dear Sir,
    I am seated in the smallest room in my house. Your critique on my last concert is in front of me. Very soon it will be behind me.

Yours truly,
Max Reger

Reger, your music sounds just like your name. Read it forward or backward, and it sounds just the same.

ANONYMOUS

The time will come when we shall begin to hear clearly enough to keep what is worth listening to, and throw away what isn't. [Oh, yeah? Deems, you dream.]

DEEMS TAYLOR IN *THE WELL-TEMPERED LISTENER*

Music is not like wine. It does not improve with age. It is either good or it is bad.

ARTURO TOSCANINI

What a critic said about Leonie Rysanek at her opening of the rebuilt Vienna Opera, 'What a pity. She has brilliant top and beautiful tessitura up there, but if she comes down in the middle, her voice sounds like an airplane that moves in the fog.

ROBERT JACOBSON

One good thing about modern music is that if you make a mistake, no one notices.

GORDON BROWN

*Andrea Chénier* exudes... all the tricks and all the banalities of Italian opera at its worst.

ERNEST NEWMAN [DE GUSTIBUS..]

One movement of a symphony, developing two themes, may last twelve or fourteen minutes. In that... time Verdi or Puccini would have got rid of two arias, a duet, and a short scene, employing... eight main and subordinate themes.

DEEMS TAYLOR

...*Tristan und Isolde.* It was years before I could sit through the second act without falling asleep... Now ... I know the first act almost by heart, I can really hear the second act ... last year I even heard the third act.

DEEMS TAYLOR

... applause at a Verdi opera, especially in the earlier ones, before Giuseppe began to have esthetic scruples, has been more or less predetermined by the composer.

DEEMS TAYLOR

... when (Georgette) Leblanc had studied *Carmen* in Granada with a gypsy, she acquired every authentic element, including fleas.

QUAINTANCE EATON, OPERA HISTORIAN

He lacked the elegance, the grace, the adroitness and the magnetic charm that the part necessitated.

LAWRENCE GILMAN OF THE *HERALD TRIBUNE*
ON PINZA'S FIRST *DON GIOVANNI*

Critics can't even make music by rubbing their back legs together.

MEL BROOKS

Despicable and the music mostly beneath contempt.

ERNEST NEWMAN ON *LA GIOCONDA*

Dame Kiri Te Kanawa is a viable alternative to valium.

IRA STEIFF

The tenor in *Die Meistersinger* sang so badly that in all fairness Beckmesser should have been acclaimed as the winner and awarded Eva's hand in wedlock. That this did not happen suggested that the jury may have been bribed.

AUTHOR UNKNOWN

A heap of mastadon droppings.

CRITIQUE OF A NEW OPERA AT CAMBRIDGE UNIVERSITY

[Richard] Strauss's music is aesthetically criminal.

ANONYMOUS

*Don Carlo* is a sprawling, five-act opera that can seem to go on forever when placed in the wrong hands.

LON TUCK IN THE *WASHINGTON POST*

The score was machine made from beginning to end, and constructed in such a way that it was tuneless and unvocal for the singers.

WILLIAM J. HENDERSON, *NEW YORK SUN*
MUSIC CRITIC ON *DON CARLO*

Be it in the opera house or the concert room, I would in nineteen cases out of twenty abide by the verdict or accepted opinion of a great orchestra far more confidently than I would that of either the press or the public.

SIR THOMAS BEECHAM

Critics are like eunuchs in a harem. They're there every night, they see how it should be done every night, but they can't do it themselves.

BRENDAN BEHAN IN *STRIKING BACK AT CRITICS*

Her voice was as beautiful as a middle-priced kazoo.

THE EDITOR

... a legendary telecast of *La Boheme* with Renata Scotto and Luciano Pavarotti, whose epic embraces one critic compared to two dumplings in love.

DAVID GOCKLEY

I once received the following note from a farmer.
Dear Sir, I wish to inform you that the man who played the long thing you pull in and out did so only during the brief periods you were looking at him.

ARTURO TOSCANINI

# MANAGERS, MONEY AND MALARKEY

I agreed to pay all their (the opera singers') traveling expenses and hotel bills, provided they would sing a few times in New Orleans and Vera Cruz, to remunerate me. Every prima donna found the necessity of bringing with her, her aunt, sister, grandmamma, or her protector, without counting for her lap-dogs or her parrots; and each tenor carrying with him his *protégée* and his servant.

MAX MARETZEK IN *REVELATIONS OF AN OPERA MANAGER IN AMERICA* (1855)

Gatti-Casazza [manager of the Metropolitan Opera] was aloof with all of us as a way of keeping above the battles of ambition and clashes of temperament that rage forever in the opera world.

EZIO PINZA

Before I became a singer's agent I had six theories on how to handle manic singers. Now I have six manic singers as clients and no theories.

ANONYMOUS

[chorus members at La Scala] are subject to the quaintest regulations which specify that they must be paid extra when wearing armour.

ANTONIO GUARNIERI, CONDUCTOR

A real impresario never pays any one!

ALFREDO SALMAGGI, A BROOKLYN IMPRESARIO WHO HAD MANY SINGERS PAY FOR THE PRIVILEGE OF SINGING IN HIS THEATER

Miss Tebaldi sang with you last season, didn't she? And I know what you paid her. And I always get much more than Miss Tebaldi.

MARIA CALLAS

This is musical piracy!
GIACOMO PUCCINI BEMOANING THE FACT, COMPOSERS RECEIVE NO ROYALTIES FOR PERFORMANCES OR RECORDINGS, WHEREAS A PRIMA DONNA OR LEAD TENOR, OFTEN MAKE MORE MONEY IN ONE EVENING THAN THE COMPOSER IS PAID FOR RIGHTS TO HIS ENTIRE OPERA

The most beautiful music is that made by coinage.

GIACOMO PUCCINI

Why shouldn't these remarkable artists earn as much as they can? None of them is in it for art alone. They are all up to their high C's in the lusts and greeds of the marketplace.

HERBERT BRESLIN, PAVAROTTI'S MANAGER

General managers can never figure out exactly what they want: polite technicians who always show up and sing the notes, or festive monsters of egotism who drive them nuts but create a buzz at the box office.

MANUELA HOELTERHOFF

Adelina Patti made her first appearance in public under my own direction in a concert in Trippler Hall... in February, 1852. She was then a child of about nine years, and at that early age not only gave evidence of her precocity in vocalizing, but also in making bargains. The conditions on which she agreed to sing then were a hatful of candies, and she insisted upon receiving it before she went out to appear before the public..

MAX MARETZEK IN *SHARPS AND FLATS*

No goddam dollars, no Götterdämmerung!

J. B. STEANE IN *SINGERS OF THE CENTURY*

I am convinced that Maria's troubles began when she started receiving ten thousand dollars a performance. That's when she started buckling under the pressure.

GUISEPPE DI STEFANO, REFERRING TO CALLAS

No one is good at everything. The challenge of a career is finding a very small number of roles you're good at. I'm of the opinion there is something good about being a great Verdi tenor, a great bel canto soprano.

MATTHEW EPSTEIN, SINGERS' MANAGER

[Musicians] talk of nothing but money and jobs. Give me businessmen every time. They really are interested in music and art.

JEAN SIBELIUS QUOTED IN *THE WELL-TEMPERED LISTENER*

I turned her down at an audition and couldn't regret it more, because if I would have had her at that time she wouldn't have been so expensive.

RUDOLF BING ON WHY HE DIDN'T
HIRE HER [CALLAS] IN THE EARLY 50'S

You know me. Nothing will separate me from my fee.

PATRICIA RACETTE, SOPRANO

I, not you, am the manager of this company, and the critics and public will hold *me* accountable if this girl [Ponselle] fails... If she is a success, the doors of the Metropolitan will be opened to other American singers because she will have made it possible.

UMBERTO GATTI-CASAZZA TO CARUSO

In opera companies the decision makers know that, aside from attending a performance and hearing recordings, there are several other ways to get a line on a singer they've never heard: first ask the singer for some printed reviews — those critiques will probably overstate the artist's strengths; second, ask the artist's rivals for their opinions — their remarks will overstate any weaknesses.

THE EDITOR

A voice was overheard at the Met behind a door marked private:　　　JOSEPH VOLPE

You want WHO to conduct this production? Have you lost your #% mind! Fergetaboutit! We had that fathead before and we nearly lost our shirts! Look — that %$# can go across the plaza, do a pair of rehearsals — a couple of concerts — takes four, maybe five days max! — and pockets 50 bills! When you call his silly-%$ agent and tell the guy you want him for SIX WEEKS the #$ just gets out his calculator and starts multiplying. It's a #% number even Carl Sagan couldn't pronounce! Gimme- abreak! Another thing, you think this guy could ever get his royal $# down to the coaching rooms to work with the singers! Last time he only coached ........ and that was only because of her big ........... s! When he's not in the house, he's in his hotel room on the horn with his dumb &# Generalintendant for &#% hours! Then he talks to his girl friends, boy friends, hangers-on and anyone else he can think of... and who pays the bill? — WE DO!

Then he wants his last piece of tail to sing one of the principal roles! Then the %#$-hole thinks he knows more about lighting than our guy! Next he'll probably want a #% flugelhorn! What the &#$ is a flugelhorn anyway?! Trying to keep your money from flying out the window in this looney bin is &% impossible! Hell, even the #$ counter-tenors want big bucks now! Alice...get ...........'s agent on the phone, pronto! He's cheap and always available and doesn't try to give us a $# each time he's here. And... Jimmy... next time, PLEASE make an appointment!"

[Entirely made up... of course! Joey... we all love you!)

FRANK CADENHEAD, PARIS

*Martha* by Flotow, *The Prophet* by Meyerbeer, and *Attila* by Verdi — three opera never heard in Mexico — formed the basis of our operations [in 1864] The principal success and attraction financially was the skating scene in *The Prophet* and the introduction of roller skating into Mexico. Skating was a new revelation to the majority of Mexicans, who knew it only from hearsay, and speedily became the rage... Roller skates and skating lessons brought enormous prices: skating clubs were formed in every class of society, and each club in rotation asked, and paid for, the privilege of showing their skill during the performance to their friends, who filled the house, and thus the Gran Teatro Nacional in Mexico, became a well-paying skating hall, with performances of Meyerbeer's *The Prophet* thrown in as an additional entertainment for the price of admisssion.

MAX MARETZEK IN *SHARPS AND FLATS* (1890)

# Is Opera going to the Dogs

Your editors and members of the New York Opera Forum plus the OPERA-L e-mail group had a romp thinking up doggone concoctions:
Arfeo and Euridice by Arfenbark
The Barkerole, also by Arfenbark
Corgi and Bess
The Mastiffsingers
The Flying Dachshund
The Dalmation of Faust
The Devil and Spaniel Webster
The Dance of the Seven Airdales
The Barker of Seville
The Marriage of Fido
Rover et Juiliette
Fido and Aeneas
The Saint Bernard of Bleeker Street
Amelia Goes to the Dogs
I Puri Cani
L'Amico Spitz
Tannschnauzer
The Golden Mongrel
Lassie of Lammermoor
Mastiff-off-the-Leash by Arf-eego Bow-eeto
Le Cur Espaniel
The Grrr of the Golden West, obviously by Pooch-eenee
Die Frau ohne Schnauzer
Borzoi Godunov

Now switching to a horse of an entirely different pastel
A Mule and the Night Visitors
Donkey Shot
Nagbucko

# Don Marty, The Ultimate Impresario

[In the late 1840s] the only regular Italian opera, save our own in New York, was located in Havana, under the direction of Don Francisco Marty y Torrens. Señor Marty belongs to the class of successful operatic Managers. The reason for this is Marty has by no means made it his principal business. But now, you will ask me about the business of the very worthy Don Marty. It is said that in his younger days, this Havanese impresario was the mate of a most formidable Pirate who infested the Mexican Gulf and the seas adjacent to it. The Spanish government offered a large recompense for the capture of this Pirate. Immediately, the youthful Francisco felt it was his duty to serve his government. The rover fell into a trap, which was very neatly laid, and was taken. He was, of course "garoted," a particularly agreeable and expeditious way of throttling a prisoner in public, which is in vogue in Cuba.

As his recompense, the amiable Francisco received the privilege of all the fish markets in the Island. Nobody in all Cuba had the right of selling a single fish, without paying certain dues to Don Francisco Marty y Torrens.

In addition to this, he had money. How much and where acquired, no one knows. This loose cash he invested in building or chartering some hundreds of fishing boats. He was therefore enabled, after a short time, to supply his own markets. This business soon took under his management such colossal proportions, that its annual profits were estimated at 10,000 ounces of gold. Retaining a certain predilection for his old profession, he fitted out several large vessels to carry on the slave trade. His baits were now fire-arms, doubloons and kegs of brandy. His hooked fish were negroes from the coast of Africa, and Indians from Yucatan. Don Marty's fortune soon reached fabulous proportions. He now dabbled in government securities, and was several times enabled to help the government of Spain out of its momentary embarrassments. For his devotion, an equivalent had to be received, and it was offered him in the shape of knighthood and "letters of nobility".

Thus he became not only powerful in Havana, but great also in Madrid. But in spite of his wealth, his power and his influence, Marty was not liked. The proud Castillian noblesse of the Island absolutely refused to tolerate the slave-dealer and fish-seller in their society. He therefore determined upon forcing them to swallow the fish.

To do this he built a splendid opera house, engaged a first-rate Opera troupe, and became his own manager. At first, lovers of song as all Spaniards are, they refused to patronize him.

Enraged at this, Don Francisco committed an act, the egotism of which was so intense, that it almost amounts to genius. He closed the doors of the Tacon theatre upon the public but retained the company. The performances were continued for himself.

There he sat, but for a few friends, in solitary grandeur, listening to and enjoying the music, almost alone. It strikes me that the grand cynicism of this conduct has never been equaled. For this alone I almost venerate the Señor Francisco Marty y Torrens.

However, the artists made acquaintances, and these acquaintances wished to hear them in Opera.

Marty heard it, and doubtless chuckled inwardly. Externally, he was inexorable.

This strange, and unaccountable behavior, raised their curiosity to the highest pitch. After interposing many insurmountable difficulties, Marty consented to treat with the aristocracy of the Cuban capital. Provided a number of them would buy up the boxes of his house for a certain series of years, and provided they would make up a purse each season, for the management, he was willing to throw open the doors of the Tacon, and furnish first-class Operatic performances. As the Spanish Señoritas are exceedingly fond of music, and even more partial to display, the Spanish Señores were obliged, by the love of melody and the terror of their better halves, to comply with these terms. Don Francisco had won his first battle with the Havana aristocracy.

Thanks, therefore, to the subscription and the compulsory subvention, which sometimes amounted to $30,000, Italian Opera flourished in Havana.

How much Marty himself understood of those musical matters on which, for a time, he had chosen to sit as the sole judge, you will allow me to retell to you an anecdote, which has been given me as perfectly true.

Sitting once, during an operatic performance, in the first row of seats, near the Orchestra, he remarked a horn-player was looking as his music without playing. For a time, the profoundly scientific Manager endured this, but when some twenty bars had passed, without bringing any signs of life into the instrument, he at last lost his patience, and turned to the unlucky horn-player - "Why the deuce don't you play, sir?" he exclaimed.

"Señor...." Queried the instrumentalist.

"Why don't you play?"

"Señor, I am counting my bars, now."

"Are you, you lazy scoundrel? Counting your bars, indeed! Why did you not count them before this?"

"I am waiting before I begin, Señor!" said the unlucky musician, in a marked tremolo.

"Begin at once!" quoth Marty.

"Señor — ? Began the man imploringly.

"Begin!" repeated the impresario,"or, when pay-day comes, I shall count my dollars and wait before I pay you."

The threat was sufficient. The horn was raised to this musician's mouth, but no sooner was the first note blown, than the Conductor turned on the instrumentalist with a savage look. The brazen tube dropped from his mouth, and then only was Don Marty aware of the error which he had made. As the audience noted what had passed with the usual quickness of Southern musical intuition, they applauded the unlucky horn. Daggers were looked at Marty by the incensed conductor.

For the winter months his company played here in New York in Castle Garden Opera House.

In the summer of 1850, Marty sent to this city the greatest troupe which had ever been heard in America. Indeed, in point of integral talent, number and excellence of the artists composing it, it must be admitted that it has seldom been excelled in any part of the Old World. The company created a profound sensation in New York.

[Editors'comment: this chapter was excerpted in abbreviated form from *Revelations of an Opera Manager in America* by Max Maretzek [1855], and his revelations are indeed hilarious. So, an ex-pirate, fish monger, slave trader and musical ignoramus was able to advance fine opera and become, for a while, the best impresario and producer in the Western Hemisphere.]

# ZANY MISCELLANY

## HOW MUCH DO YOU WEIGH?

A friend:    How much do you weigh?
Pavarotti:   Less than before.
A friend:    How much did you weigh before?
Pavarotti:   More than now.

*THE PRIVATE LIVES OF THE THREE TENORS* BY MARCIA LEWIS

He eats to relax... It's just another reflection of Luciano's great appetite for life. He is not a moderate man.

MRS. ADUA PAVAROTTI

A violin can't be a little tiny thing and produce a great sound. Important voices usually go with an important body (I will avoid saying the fat body).

LUCIANO PAVAROTTI

Audiences... seem to be becoming less tolerant of the more grossly-overfed Bohemians at least, along with the late-middle-aged corseted Siegfrieds, Teutons, Carmens, the Ebolis and Turandots whose *'don fatale'* [fatal gift] poses the most minimal of threats.

MEIRION AND SUSIE HARRIES IN *OPERA TODAY*

... the fat singer is not always the undramatic singer and to a producer the capacity to feel and convey emotion on stage may be worth far more than the authentic face and figure of a courtesan or toreador or wood nymph.

IBID

Some gotta da figure, I gotta da voice.

FAT LITTLE DIVA LUISA TETRAZZINI

... French soprano Amelia Talexis in 1911, on a trip to England, stayed in a hotel in Calais. Talexis was so heavy, the porcelain commode she was sitting on collapsed. She bled to death from the injuries she sustained.

ROBERT BAXTER

## A CONCERT PROGRAM SEQUENCE IN BOSTON

*Le Coq d'Or*
*The Golden Cock*          Nikolay Rimsky-Korsakov
*Le Dernier Sommeil d'une Vierge*
*The Last Sleep of a Virgin*  Jules Massenet
*Hänsel und Gretel*        Engelbert Humperdinck

ACCORDING TO NICHOLAS SLONIMSKY

## DAFFY DEFINITIONS

| | |
|---|---|
| Tenore di disgrazia: | A lousy tenor |
| ½ Soprano: | English for mezzo-soprano in an Italian opera program |
| Castrati: | "Singing elephants" who "get the girl, but don't know what to do with her." |
| Coloratura: | A soprano with hiccups. |
| Basso sprofondato: | A deeper voice than a basso profondo. |
| Soprano: | Generally pretty clueless, her main job is to stand around looking good while others fight over her. Sometimes gets to die in the end — tragically and at great length. |

DAVID BARBER

Mezzo-soprano: A soprano who smoked.

GEORGETTA PSAROS

Mezzo-soprano: A soprano without high notes.

LILLI LEHMANN

Sopranophilia: A common disease of conductors, voice coaches and opera buffs

A WAGNERIAN SOPRANO

Phonograph: An irritating toy that restores life to dead noises.

AMBROSE BIERCE, AMERICAN AUTHOR

Recital: A place where old opera singers go before they die.

DAVID BARBER

Toga role: A part demanding a sonorous bass voice, superior technique, and almost no acting.

ROSA PONSELLE

Most of novice singers: "Fireflies mistaken for lanterns".

THE EDITORS

## BOX OFFICE SIGNS IN ITALY

RIPOSO STASSERA.
(Translation: No Performance Tonight)
VERY SORRY WE ARE EXHAUSTED
(Translation: Sorry, we're sold out)
For the public's greater convenience spectators in the first class rows will have to get down on the floor close to each other; those in the second class section will kneel; third class ticket holders will remain seated; and those in the fourth class rows will stand. Thus every one will be able to see.

AN 1734 THEATER SIGN IN MANTOVA, ITALY, FROM *CINQUECENTO E UNA CURIOSITÀ MUSICALI* [1910], EDITED BY ADOLFO LAPPINI

## BARITONES WITH HIGH C's

Lawrence Tibbett: John, I'll bet my high C is better than
yours.
Tenor John McCormack: Let's hear it.
(Tibbett blasts out a tremendous high C)
John McCormack: Larry, that's it! But I get paid much
more for mine.

TENOR CHARLES CONTI

Caruso in his dressing room was trying over and over
the *Faust* aria phrase with the climaxing high C, but
botched the high note time after time. In the next
dressing room his pal, baritone Antonio Scotti, crooned
that tenor phrase and finished it off with a loud,
glorious high C. Caruso, furious, grabbed his wooden
make-up box, opened Scotti's door and hurled it at him.

JOHN GUALIANI

The "King of the Baritones," Titta Ruffo, on a bet
erupted with a roof-raising, interpolated high C in the
*Barber of Seville*. He held it for what one listener swore
was about 25 seconds. He won his bet, but had to rest
his throat for three days.

OLGA ISACESCU, RUFFO'S COMMON-LAW WIFE

## COSTUMES, MAKE-UP AND VELCRO

Elderly Conductor: Miss Garden, in your place, I'd
wear more clothing.
Mary Garden: (very décolleté) I'm quite ready to
believe what you say, Maestro.

FROM *OPERA ANTICS & ANECDOTES*

Without safety pins there is no opera.

SALLY AMATO [WHAT ABOUT VELCRO, SAL?]

110

Venus de Kilo's costume designer must have been Omar the Tentmaker.

THE EDITORS

She: She certainly has a wide vibrato.
He: Yeah, and that yellow dress makes it look even
    bigger.

ALBERT SCHMIDT

... a white Macbeth and a black Lady Macbeth, a white Norma and a black Adalgisa, a white Rudolfo and a black Mimi present no problem, a white Rigoletto and black Gilda, a black Daland and white Senta can, initially at least, be distracting.

MEIRION AND SUSIE HARRIES

❦

## OPERATIC DISAPPOINTMENTS

The first ballad opera composed (1767) in America was entitled (correctly). *The Disappointment* (composer unknown)... It included the song *Yankee Doodle*, also known as *The Lexington March*, adopted as America's unofficial anthem in 1782.

*THE GUINESS BOOK OF MUSIC*

For most people, a modern opera has all the appeal of a large pill that must be swallowed on the orders of an unseen sadist. That's the legacy of fifty years of music that often sounds like water drips and surgery without anesthesia

MANUELA HOELTERHOFF

Is there another art form that attracts so many sublime sufferers and so many nuts?

MANUELA HOELTERHOFF

111

This season there may be an audience for *Lakme* or *Euranthe* or *La Wally*, but how many people are going to want to see them again within the next ten or fifteen years?

MEIRION AND SUSIE HARRIES

With some it takes a few bars to determine the language, let alone the words.

MICHAEL LANGDON, HEAD OF BRITAIN'S NATIONAL OPERA STUDIO, ON DICTION

## NICKNAMES – EITHER ACCIDENTAL OR FACETIOUS

O. de Cologne (Offenbach, born in Cologne, Germany, occasionally signed thusly)
Orpheus and Uterus
Orpheus in his Underwear
La forza dell'intestino
Manon Let's Go
Der Ring der Niegelungenen
Johnny Squeaky
The Rape's Progress

## FOR THE BENEFIT OF ENGLISH SPEAKERS

The plot of *Carmen* taken from program notes at the Carlo Felice Opera House in Genoa.

Act One: Carmen, a cigarmakeress from a tobago factory loves Don Jose of the mounting guard. Carmen takes a flower from her corsets and lances it to Don Jose. (Duet: 'Talk me of my mother.') There was noise in side the tobago factory and revolting cigar-makeresses burst onto the stage. Carmen is arrested and Don Jose is ordered to mounting guard on her but she subduces him and lets her escape.

Act Two: The Tavern. Carmen sings (Aria: 'The sistrums tinkling.') Enter two smugglers ('Ho, we have in mind a business'.) Enter Escamillio, a Balls fighter. Carmen refuses to penetrate because Don Jose has liberated her from prison. He just now arrives. (Aria: 'Slop-here who comes'.) But here are the bugles singing his retreat. Don Jose will leave and draws his sword. Called by Carmen's shrieks the two smugglers interfere with her. Jose is bound to dessert. Final Chorus: "Opening Sky Wandering Life."

Act Three: A rocky landscape. Smugglers chatter. Carmen sees her death in the cards. Don Jose makes a date with her for the next Balls fight.

Act Four: A Place in Seville. Procession of Ball-fighters. The roaring of Balls is heard in the arena, Escamillio enters (Aria and chorus: 'Toreador, Toreador. All hail the Balls of a toreador.') Enter Don Jose (Aria: 'I besmooch you.') Carmen repels him. She wants to join with Escamillio now chaired by the crowd. Don Jose stabs her. (Aria: 'Oh, rupture, rupture.') He sings: "Oh, my subductive Carmen."

QUOTED FROM *THE RETURN OF HEROIC FAILURES* BY STEPHEN PILE

Do they [prompters] do something other than libretto cues?… Like signaling an unzipped zipper?

A MEMBER OF OPERA-L

THE CHORUS

Sarah Caldwell:   We're six daggers short. How can these six ladies commit suicide?
Boris Goldovsky: Zey vill drink poison from zer rrrings!

ANN STAFFELD, A MEMBER OF THE LESTROYENNES CHORUS

Ladies of the chorus, I want you to sound like twenty-two women having babies without chloroform.

SIR JOHN BARBIROLLI

Za ladies are schniffing zer bloomers too zoon.

CONDUCTOR HANS RICHTER TO THE *LOHENGRIN* BRIDAL CHORUS
RE SMELLING THEIR BOUQUETS, FROM *OPERA ANTICS & ANECDOTES*

A group of eighty or a hundred singers with messy cutoffs is a very noticeable group.

DAVID STIVENDER, CHORAL DIRECTOR

## SINGERS COMMENT ON THEIR OWN RECORDINGS

Ah! My God! Now I understand why I am Patti! Oh, yes! What a voice! What an artist! I understand it all.

ADELINA PATTI, ECSTATIC ON FIRST HEARING
HER RECORDED VOICE IN 1906

Good grief! If I sounded like that, would any one pay to hear me?

NELLIE MELBA, ON FIRST HEARING HER RECORDED VOICE

## OPERATIC SHAKESPEARE

Clearly, no dramatist wrote plots more operatic than William Shakespeare. Over one hundred composers have used his plays. One wonders if *The Winter's Tale* by Zhang Zhilling or *Much Ado about Nothing* by Chen Jing Gwen honored their composers' names onomato-poeically by featuring clashing cymbals. Then again, what about the composer with the glorious name Haack who used *The Tempest* for his opera? Did the composer's name have a negative effect on sales in English-speaking countries?

THE EDITORS

114

In 1928 too much champagne wrecked a Milan

*Traviata*, but created a new art form. It all happened at the old Dal Verme theater. In her dressing room with friends, the prima donna had fortified herself with too many glasses of bubbly. Bottle blind, she made a gawd-awful mess of the first act. What to do with no sub and a Violetta unfit to continue? The frantic manager beat his forehead to find a way, any way, to avoid refunding the ticket money.

After a long intermission, the curtains reopened and nonplussed spectators were greeted not by the second act of *La Traviata*, but the second act of *Tosca*. The listeners scratched their heads, but sat through the remainder of that opera. This improvised "opera-mixte" inspired a spoof review in a Milan periodical, *Il Meschin Guerrier,* herewith reproduced into English.

In the present era of crisis within the theater, the Dal Verme's innovation offers a series of benefits no one had thought of before: the monotony of some

115

performances is done away with, uncertainty is assured, and variety guaranteed.

Moreover, it has the advantage of making old operas young again. It could become a kind of Voronoff monkey-gland cure for the entire opera repertory.

*La Traviata* is exactly 75 years old; she carries her age well, but still she's all of 75. The management over at the Dal Verme, however, has applied its own 'cure', and now *Traviata* suddenly becomes the age of *Tosca*, which is 28.

Isn't that a prodigious feat?

One should also appreciate the management's delicacy in finding two operas with such pronounced similarities which can complement each other so excellently.

After all, *Traviata* and *Tosca* both deal with an ill-starred love which could be easily lumped together as follows:

Madamigella Violetta, who, not to slight Floria Tosca, we shall call Violettosca, falls in love with the painter, Alfredo Cavaradossi, a Roman artist, a native of Provenza il Mar, il Sol.

Violettosca, on the other hand, is a famous singer who has contracted a slight case of TB, thanks to her habit of going around the unheated churches of Rome with bare chest and bare arms. She is much loved and sought after by the Baron Scarpia-Duval, a notorious man-about-town. The latter, to satisfy his libertine lust, wins a competition and becomes the Prefect of Police of the Seine, the historic river in which Rome is mirrored, and in this capacity he has the painter Alfredo Cavaradossi arrested.

Violettosca, excessively jealous, arrives to find out why on earth her lover has been arrested. She suspects the whole business involves women.

But at this point a beautiful, very moving and unexpected event takes place. Baron Scarpia-Duval announces he is the father of the painter Alfredo Cavaradossi and that he had him arrested for purely family reasons. I fact, pure as an angel God gave him a daughter who cannot marry unless her artist brother, Alfredo Cavaradossi, gives up bad company, that is to say, unless he drops Madamigella Violettosca like a hot potato.

At this point, there is an extremely serious turn of events. The father, that is to say, Baron Scarpia-Duval, suddenly has a brillant idea how to separate the two lovers. He condemns Alfredo Cavaradossi to be executed by a firing squad, and Madamigella Violettosca to die of TB. That way it will be difficult for them to see each other again.

In the last act, as that great artist the Doctor so justly announces, since the TB only leaves her a few hours before death, Madamigella Violettosca, who is very vindictive, kills Scarpia-Duval, who is the father of her lover, and thus Alfredo Cavaradossi is forced to face the firing squad an orphan.Then Madamigella Violettosca dies of tuberculosis by hurling herself off the terrace of the Castel Sant'Angelo into the Seine.

As you can see, the two operas fit perfectly. And we want to express our gratitude to the management of the Dal Verme which knew how to blend so tactfully two scores which seemed so very dissimilar to the uninitiated.

We've learned that, to avoid any misunderstandings, and to keep the new opera-mixte the Dal Verme has cobbled together from being confused either with *La Traviata* or with *Tosca*, the management has decided — in order not to offend anybody — to call the opera *La Traviatosca*.

117

# THE FINAL CURTAIN

The custom of singers holding hands during curtain calls is a wise and logical tradition. It restrains any applause-giddy singer from lunging forward for a solo bow.

JOHN GUALIANI

Titta Ruffo: How did that exercise sound to you?
Olga Isacescu: (his companion) One note sounded bad.
Titta Ruffo: (in the 1930's) Yes! And for lack of that note, there is no more Titta Ruffo.

FROM OLGA ISACESCU TO THE EDITOR

It's time to restrict my singing to the bathroom.

BIRGIT NILSSON (1984)

Giulia, when I abandoned music, I started to die a little.

MARIA CALLAS TO GIULIETTA SIMIONATO

All the glory ends in nothing! [*La gloria finisce nel nulla*]

TITTA RUFFO, ELDERLY, DEPRESSED AND
LONELY TO THE EDITOR IN 1944

If I had to do it all over again, I'd not become a singer.
I suffered too much.

GIULIETTA SIMIONATO

Enrico Caruso died in August 1921. Titta Ruffo was
invited to sing at his funeral, but, as he told the editor,
he begged off, saying he could not sing there without
breaking into tears. Fyodor Chaliapin was also grief-
stricken, for he, Caruso and Ruffo were not only the
leading international stars in their voice categories, but
also the best of devil-may-care pals, brimming with
mutual esteem. In December 1921, for his first
performance at the Met of *Boris Godunov*, Chaliapin was
assigned Caruso's old dressing room. On the wall he
wrote in Russian, as he told Maxim Gorky, a graffito:
dedicated to Caruso which ended: "I weep, and in reply
to my memories of you, your muse is weeping softly
too."

THE EDITORS

Prima Donna Giulia Grisi has a record: her "final" stage
and concert appearances began in 1854 and lasted until
1866.

No one watches opera on the radio any more now that
we have TV.

FROM *PENTATETTE* THE LIMERICK NEWSLETTER

Let's end on a light Shakespearean note: if "all the
world's a stage,"where's the audience supposed to sit?

ENRICO CARUSO - SIR PAOLO TOSTI - ANTONIO SCOTTI
**ARRIVEDERCI! GOODBYE!**

# Index

# Bibliography

*Agitato* by Jerome Toobin, © Viking Press
*Aina on Polku Eessa* by Annukka Talvela,
© Gummerus 1999
*A Little Night Music* by Samuel Chotzinoff,
© Harper & Row 1964
*A Smattering of Ignorance* by Oscar Levant,
© American Ltd 1997
*Bartlett's Book of Anecdotes* ed. Clifton Fadiman
& Andre' Bernard, © Little, Brown and Co 1985
*Bel Canto* by Ann Patchett, © Perenniel 2002
*Beverly An Autobiography* by Beverly Sills &
Lawrence Linderman, © Bantam 1987
*Bizet and His World* by Mina Curtiss, © Venna House 1974
*Caruso The Man of Naples and the Voice of Gold*
by T. R. Ybarra, © Hartcourt Brace and Co 1953
*Chaliapin, An Autobiography, as Told to Maxim Gorky,*
ed. by Nina Froud & James Hanley, © Stein and day 1969
*Cinquecento ed una curiositá musicali*
ed. by Adolfo Lappini 1910
*Cinderella & Company* by Manuela Hoelterhoff,
© Alfred A. Knopf 1999
*Conducting: A Backwoods Guide* by David Schiff,
© *The Atlantic Monthly*
*Conductors, A New Generation* by Philip Hart,
© Charles Scribner's & Sons 1979
*Crotchets and Quavers* by Max Maretzek
© Da Capo Press 1966
*Diva – Great Sopranos and Mezzos Discuss Their Art* by
Helen Matheopoulos, © Northeastern University Press1991
*Ezio Pinza, An Autobiography* with Robert Magidoff,
© Rinehart & Company, Inc. 1958
*Gentlemen, More Dolce Please* by Harry Ellis Dickson,
Beacon Press 1969
*Greek Fire,* The Story of Maria Callas and Aristotle
Onassis, by Nicholas Gage, Knopf 2000
*A History of Russian Music* by Richard Anthony Leonard,
© Greenwood Publishing Group 1977

*Humor and Harmony* by Vladimir Cernikoff,
© Arthur Barker Ltd 1936
*Life with Luciano* by Mrs. Adua Pavarotti, © Allen & Unwin
*Love Lives of the Great Composers* by Basil Howitt,
© Sound And Vision 1995
*Maestro, Encounters With Conductors of Today*
by Helena Matheopoulos, © Hutchinson 1982
*Maria Callas The Woman behind the Legend*
By Arianna Stassinopoulos, © Ballantine Books 1982
*Memoirs* by Sir Georg Solti, © Knopf 1997
*Memoirs of Lorenzo Da Ponte.* Translated from the Italian
by Elisabeth Abbott, © Dover Publications 1929
*More Love Lives of the Great Composers,* by Basil Howitt,
© Sound And Vision 2002
*My Road to Opera* by Boris Goldovsky, © Houghton Mifflin
Company, Boston 1979
*Opera* by Edward J. Dent, © Penguin Books 1940
*Opera – A Concise History* by Leslie Orrey & Rodney Milnes,
© Thames and Hudson 1987
*Opera Antics & Anecdotes* by Stephen Tanner,
© Sound And Vision 1999
*Opera for Dummies* by David Poque and Scott Speck,
© John Wiley & Sons 1997
*Opera Offstage* by Milton Brener, © Walker Publishing
Co. 1996
*Opera Small Talk* by Robert Levine & Elizabeth Lutyens,
© Cherubino Press 1993
*Opera Today* by Meirion & Susan Harries,
© St. Martin's Press 1986
*Pavarotti My Own Story* with William Wright,
© Doubleday & Compapny 1981
*Pentatette, a limerick newsletter,* edited and produced by
Dr. Arthur Deex, Moffett, California
*Placido Domingo's Tales from the Opera* by Daniel
Snowman, © BBC Publications 1994
*Ponselle a Singer's Life* by Rosa Ponselle &
James A. Drake, © Doubleday 1982

*Renata Tebaldi The Voice of an Angel* by Carlamaria Casanova, © Baskerville Publishers 1995

*Revelations of an Opera Manager in America* by Max Maretzek (1855), ©DaCapo 1966

*Reverberations, Interviews with the World's Leading Musicians* by Robert Jacobson, © William Morrow 1974

*Striking Back at Critics* by Peter Hay in *Performing Arts*

*The American Opera Singer* by Peter G. Davis © Doubleday 1997

*The Bluebird of Happiness The Memoirs of Jan Peerce* by Alan Levy, © Harper & Row 1976

*The Boston Opera Company 1909-1916* by Quaintance Eaton © Appleton-Century 1965

*The Book of Musical Anecdotes* by Norman Lebrecht, © The Free Press 1985

*The Met* by Martin Mayer, © Simon & Schuster 1983

*The Metropolitan Opera Encyclopedia* edited by David Hamilton, © Simon & Schuster

*The Mingled Chime* by Sir Thomas Beecham © Hutchinson 1948

*The Magic of the Opera* by Mary Ellis Peltz, © Frederick A. Prager, Inc 1960

*The Private Lives of the Three Tenors* by Marcia Lewis, © Birch Lane Press 1996

*The Return of Heroic Failures* by Stephen Pile, © Secker & Warburg 1988

*The Tenors*, edited by Herbert Breslin, © MacMillan 1974

*The Well Tempered Listener* by Deems Taylor, © Simon & Schuster 1943

*The Verdi-Boito Correspondence*, edited by William Weaver, © University of Chicago Press 1994

*Verdi* by John Rosselli, © Cambridge University Press 2000

*Warten auf's hohe C,* by Alexander Witeschnik, © Neff Verlag Wien

*What Time's The Next Swan?* by Walter Slezak © Doubleday 1962

*Which Reminds Me* by Tony Randall, © Delacorte Press 1989

# Acknowledgements

So many of our best quotes were told to us by friends and acquaintances active in music that we want to name them and thank them by name. Gemma Bosini, Frank Cadenhead, Charles Conti, James Craven, Mario del Monaco, Quaintance Eaton, Gigliola Galli. John Gualiani. Vera Smirnova Henkel, Olga Isacescu, Elwood McKee, Arturo Merlini, Kari Nurmela, Jef Olson, G. Paul Padillo, Georgetta Psaros, Robert Ridout, Titta Ruffo, Bob Salmon, Albert Schmidt, Rudolf Schneider, Paolo Silveri, Ann Staffeld, Lynne Strow, Martti Talvela, Michel Tapin, Emma Walters, Gail White and Orville White.

Editorial and artwork help from Bruce Surtees and Norman Graber enhanced greatly the quality of our book, as did our ultra-patient, energetic publisher Geoffrey Savage of Sound And Vision.

The Editors have made substantial efforts both to credit persons who gave them quotes and to identify and credit authors and publishers of previously printed items. They welcome information about any omissions or errors so corrections can be made in later printings.

The black and white photos of Caruso, Tosti and Scotti at the beginning and end of the book were snapped on a Kodak Brownie camera in Sorrento, Italy around 1911. The photographer was the great diva Adelina Patti who was driving by in her carriage.

Steve & Nancy Tanner<br>
Vermont

## The Editors

Both editors began their entrancement with opera in the early 1930s. Nancy Tanner in college took supernumerary jobs with various New York opera companies and, as a flutist, played in chamber music and opera orchestras in Germany and Italy. Steve began voice lessons in 1940 and still warbles in concerts and churches. (He lost his amateur status in Heidelberg, Germany when some one offered him money if he would agree *not* to sing.)

Steve began seriously palling around and singing with opera folk also in 1940. Sound And Vision published in 1999 a treasure trove of backstage opera humor collected by Steve and called *Opera Antics & Anecdotes*. As of 2003, aside from *Quotable Opera*, he has penned a book of international tourist humor entitled *Global Travel Laughs — Tit Bites Florentine*.

The Editors are 80 and 76 year old and have musical tastes that lean toward the 18th and 19th centuries more than to the 21st.

## The Illustrator

Umberto Tàccola is an all-around artist, burdened with the same age and demented sense of humor as Steve. He now lives in Isernia, Italy. Previously, he made a name for himself in Canada where he is a citizen. He produced graphic art, paintings (including one on commission for Vice President Nelson Rockefeller), sculpture, poetry, newspaper articles, stage plays, radio and TV. It's hard to be more versatile than that!

Other Quotable Books

*Quotable War Or Peace*
Compiled & Edited by Geoff Savage
Caricatures by Mike Rooth
isbn 0-920151-57-4

*Quotable Pop*
Fifty Decades of Blah Blah Blah
Compiled & Edited by Phil Dellio & Scott Woods
Caricatures by Mike Rooth
isbn 0-920151-50-7

*Quotable Jazz*
Compiled & Edited by Marshall Bowden
Caricatures by Mike Rooth
isbn 0-920151-55-8

*Quotable Alice*
Compiled & Edited by David W. Barber
Illustrations by Sir John Tenniel
isbn 0-920151-52-3

*Quotable Sherlock*
Compiled & Edited by David W. Barber
Illustrations by Sidney Paget
isbn 0-920151-53-1

*Quotable Twain*
Compiled & Edited by David W. Barber
isbn 0-920151-56-6

Books by David W. Barber & Dave Donald:

*A Musician's Dictionary*
preface by Yehudi Menuhin
isbn 0-920151-21-3

*Bach, Beethoven and the Boys*
Music History as It Ought to Be Taught
preface by Anthony Burgess
isbn 0-920151-10-8

*When the Fat Lady Sings*
Opera History as It Ought to Be Taught
preface by Maureen Forrester
foreword by Anna Russell
isbn 0-920151-34-5

*If It Ain't Baroque*
More Music History as It Ought to Be Taught
isbn 0-920151-15-9

*Tenors, Tantrums and Trills*
An Opera Dictionary from Aida to Zzzz
isbn 0-920151-19-1

*Tutus, Tights and Tiptoes*
Ballet History as It Ought to Be Taught
preface by Karen Kain
isbn 0-920151-30-2

*Better Than It Sounds*
A Dictionary of Humorous Musical Quotations
isbn 0-920151-22-1
Compiled & Edited by
David W. Barber

*The Music Lover's Quotation Book*
isbn 0-920151-37-X
Compiled & Edited by
David W. Barber

*The Composers*
A Hystery of Music
by Kevin Reeves
preface by Daniel Taylor
isbn 0-920151-29-9

*1812 And All That*
A Concise History of Music from 30.000 BC
to the Millennium
by Lawrence Leonard,
cartoons by Emma Bebbington
isbn 0-920151-33-7

*How to Stay Awake*
During Anybody's Second Movement
by David E. Walden, cartoons by Mike Duncan
preface by Charlie Farquharson
isbn 0-920151-20-5

*How To Listen To Modern Music*
Without Earplugs
by David E. Walden, cartoons by Mike Duncan
foreword by Bramwell Tovey
isbn 0-920151-31-0

*The Thing I've Played With the Most*
Professor Anthon E. Darling Discusses
His Favourite Instrument
by David E. Walden, cartoons by Mike Duncan
foreword by Mabel May Squinnge, B.O.
isbn 0-920151-35-3

*Love Lives of the Great Composers*
From Gesualdo to Wagner
by Basil Howitt
isbn 0-920151-18-3

*More Love Lives of the Great Composers*
by Basil Howitt
isbn 0-920151-36-1

*Opera Antics & Annecdotes*
by Stephen Tanner
Illustrations by Umberto Tàccola
preface by David W. Barber
isbn 0-920151-32-9

*I Wanna Be Sedated*
Pop Music in the Seventies
by Phil Dellio & Scott Woods
Caricatures by Dave Prothero
preface by Chuck Eddy
isbn 0-920151-16-7

*A Working Musician's Joke Book*
by Daniel G. Theaker
Cartoons by Mike Freen
preface by David Barber
isbn o-920151-23-X

First published in Canada by
**Sound And Vision**
359 Riverdale Avenue
Toronto, Canada, M4J 1A4
www.soundandvision.com
First printing, July 2003
1 3 5 7 9 - printings - 10 8 6 4 2

**National Library of Canada Cataloguing in
Publication Data**
Quotable opera / compiled & edited by
Steve and Nancy Tanner. (Quotable books)
Caricatures by Umberto Tàccola. Includes index.
ISBN 0-920151-54-X
1. Opera—Quotations, maxims, etc. I. Tanner,
Stephen II. Tanner, Nancy
III. Tàccola, Umberto, IV. Series.
ML1700.Q92 2003      782.1      C2002-904224-0


Typeset in ITC Palatino
Printed and bound in Canada by Metrolitho Inc

# Note from the Publisher

Sound And Vision books may be purchased for educational or promotional use or for special sales. If you have any comments on this book or any other books we publish, or if you would like a catalogue, please write to us at Sound And Vision 359 Riverdale Avenue, Toronto, Canada M4J 1A4.

We are always looking for original books to publish. If you have an idea or manuscript that is in the genre of musical humour including educational themes, please contact us. Thank you for purchasing or borrowing this book.

Our mandate has always been to publish books for the international market and also to sell foreign rights. I have been successful over the years in finding European publishers who have successfully translated a number of our titles. This year I'm pleased to see our books are being translated and published in China.

To view our catalogue online, please visit us at: www.soundandvision.com.

Geoffrey Savage
*Publisher*